Teaching With Trauma in Mind
Teaching Black and Poor Students More Effectively by Being Trauma-Informed

© Joseph and Zakia Gibson, 2019

ISBN 978-0-9980645-1-2

Published, printed, and distributed by:

Pathways Global Press, LLC
pathwaysinstitutes.com

In partnership with KITABU Publishing, LLC

For more information on ordering this title or to check author availability for Professional Learning Workshops for your school, district, or ISD, please contact Zakia Gibson at 313-355-0952 or zgibson@pathwaysinstitutes.org.

Zakia's Dedication

For the students and youth whose paths I've been fortunate to cross on this life's journey, Norena Fohsta, Nicole Dobbs, Lashanda Turner and hundreds more. You have learned you are not your trauma. I will always be thankful for what I learned from you! I am proud of you for being stronger than your trauma and I am honored you shared your stories with me and allowed me to help you heal. You are brilliant and talented and will not only survive, but truly live your life and create a greater legacy!

To my devoted teacher and school leader mentees and friends Felicia Brimage, Stephanie Nimene, and Stephanie Hines-Smith. You are passionate and dynamic leaders. Your commitment to education and children is relentless and highly respected. Trauma alters the discovery of life purpose. Children are resilient. Continue to support children with restoring their naturally creative genius. Identify. Connect. Empathize. Support OUR CHILDREN in their evolution to reunite with their true potential. Remember, we are advocates for children. This begins with Teaching and Leading with Trauma in Mind. The baton has been passed to you, WIN!

Joseph's Dedication

I dedicate this work to my awesome wife, who has experienced trauma's impact on education from all possible perspectives with courage and compassion. She is the first trauma-informed educator I have ever known intimately. I'm extremely proud of the phenomenal woman you've become. Thank you for loving me.

Teaching With Trauma in Mind is also dedicated to Pete Trammell, Aaron Davis, Shayne Thomas, and Don Williams. During our limited time together, you all have distinctly touched my spirit and impacted how I'll forever respond to trauma both as an educator and as a man. Despite your individual experiences with trauma, you guys have become more powerful than you even realize and destined for success. "The victim," to quote James Baldwin, "who is able to articulate the situation of the victim has ceased to be a victim: he or she has become a threat."

"Focusing on academics while struggling with trauma is like trying to play chess in a hurricane."

-Ray Wolpow

176   Holding Fast to a Doomed Fly's Wings
Why Knowing Trauma Is Not an Excuse for "Bad" Students (and Not Knowing Trauma Doesn't Excuse "Bad" Teaching)

Where the Wound Was Made[1]

An Introduction to Childhood Trauma-based Neuroplasticity and the Significance of Being a Trauma-Informed Teacher in Today's High-Poverty, High-Minority Classrooms

"The greatest hope for traumatized children is to receive a good education in schools where they are seen and known, where they learn to regulate themselves, and where they can develop a sense of agency."

-Bessel van der Kolk

"Children learn more from what you are than what you teach."

-W.E.B. DuBois

"Few events outside the classroom have as profound an impact on multiple domains of student development as traumatic life experiences," explained Isaiah Pickens and Nicole Tschopp. Numerous studies have confirmed that childhood trauma can terribly undermine a student's ability to behave appropriately and achieve their academic potential; thus, teachers must at least be familiar with (and preferably proficient in) strategies designed to mitigate trauma's impact in the classroom.

---

[1] Excerpted from the following Alice Walker quote from *The Way Forward Is with a Broken Heart*: "Healing begins where the wound was made."

About five years ago, the National Task Force on Children Exposed to Violence recommended (or perhaps more accurately, warned) that "every school in our country should have trauma-informed staff and consultants providing school-based trauma-specific treatment." Apparently, few schools—especially those with high-poverty, high-minority student populations—actually heard (and heeded) the recommendation.

However, most teachers and school administrators (we refer to both groups throughout the book as *educators*) have accepted that there is simply not enough time to focus on "soft skills" like teaching impulse control, resilience, or emotional regulation and concurrently cover enough content to get test scores high enough to maintain their employment. Our rebuttal to this conclusion is that time isn't their problem, values and priorities are. In other words, if being a trauma-informed educator was adequately valued, then it would be prioritized and time would be "found" to be a trauma-informed educator.

It's understandably difficult to value or prioritize something you know very little about. Ask most urban teachers or school administrators what it means to be "trauma-informed," and they'll probably stumble through some impromptu, inaccurately deduced response rather than rattle off some internalized version of the Substance Abuse and Mental Health Services Administration's (SAMHSA) definition. This definition, by the way, is that an individual, "program, organization, or system that is trauma-informed: *realizes* the widespread impact of trauma and understands potential paths for recovery; *recognizes* the signs and symptoms of trauma in clients, families, staff, and others involved with the system; *responds* by fully integrating knowledge about trauma into policies, procedures, and practices; and seeks to actively resist *re-traumatization*."

Being trauma-informed means enthusiastically changing how we perceive students and react to their negative classroom behaviors. It's means, explained Sandra Bloom, learning and adopting strategies that enable us to shift the basis of our response from "what is wrong with you?" to "what happened to you and how can I help?" when addressing disruptive or self-handicapping student behavior.

Becoming trauma-informed also requires a fundamental understanding that trauma, to quote Catherine Woodiwiss, "permanently changes us." Specifically, the chronic stress accompanying ongoing (or complex) childhood trauma can negatively and enduringly change a child's brain. Childhood traumas like physical or emotional abuse, sexual assault, and persistent family poverty typically triggers *neuroplasticity* (another far too uncommon term among today's urban educators).

The human brain, explained Arnulf Kolstad, "adjusts to the environment, the social situation, and to our psychological reactions. The brain develops new capacity as a result of our experience, our physical and mental activity, and how we cope with the situation. It stores what happens and creates new ways of thinking, feeling, and behaving. This quality of the brain is due to its 'plasticity,' or ability to develop and change. Physical and mental activity produces structural changes in the brain due to the brain plasticity in humans." Neural pathways and structures (e.g., prefrontal cortex, hippocampus, and amygdala) are maladaptively changed as the brain is burdened by being constantly forced to adapt to abnormally recurrent adverse physical or psychosocial situations like childhood trauma.

Students impacted by childhood trauma tend to struggle with regulating negative emotions and impulsivity as well as overcoming their overreliance on self-handicapping academic behaviors. They tend to disproportionately engage in disruptive classroom antics, apathy, absenteeism, noncompliance, incompetence, excuses, vulgarity, and misplaced aggression. Oftentimes, school gradually stops being understood as a priority for students experiencing childhood trauma; survival, or rather, somehow dealing the fear of not surviving, semiconsciously becomes too much of a priority.

These students rarely consciously "choose to behave differently," Eric Jensen explained, "but they are faced daily with overwhelming challenges that [untraumatized] children never have to confront, and their brains have adapted to suboptimal conditions in ways that undermine good school performance." Their brains have maladapted (i.e., negatively changed) in order to simply survive past and ongoing circumstances, most of which are uncontrollable, negative, and unpredictable (i.e., traumatic).

Unfortunately, childhood trauma isn't typically perceived or responded to the same in high-poverty, high-minority schools as it is in more affluent, majority-White schools. There's a greater reluctance to be trauma-informed among the instructional staff serving the former because the negative classroom behaviors of Black and/or poor students[2] are automatically seen as confirmation of stigma-based expectations rather than consequences of *trauma-based maladaptive neuroplasticity* (which is basically a fancy way of saying experiencing trauma has negatively changed how your brain looks and/or works). Fortunately, this reaction can be acknowledged and successfully modified.

Understanding at least the basics of childhood trauma and how trauma-based maladaptive neuroplasticity can evolve is the first

---

[2] This book focuses on the uniqueness of childhood trauma experienced by African-American and/or poor students, how these experiences leads to specific brain changes and classroom behaviors, and how their teachers could more strategically manage those changes and behaviors. Few, if any, books addressing childhood trauma's impact in the classroom focus on this particular subgroup, and none that we've seen consider contemporary racism (and racial stigma) as a pervasive source of complex (ongoing) trauma distinctively impacting African-American youth. I'm (Joe) especially attentive to the Black experience in America; it's what I have written about almost exclusively throughout my career. We also know that it's still relatively underexplored with regard to certain topics (this being one of them). However, most of the content throughout *Teaching With Trauma in Mind* is applicable to all students, especially those from any stigmatized group.

step of knowing how to support those students whose classroom behaviors indicate the possibility of traumatization.

There are quite a few research and practice-based actionable strategies teachers and administrators can employ when working with students that are possibly traumatized. Many of them can produce positive neuroplasticity, which can reverse many of the negative changes (maladaptive neuroplasticity) imposed on a student's brain by childhood trauma. The intentional "positivity of the school and the neuroplasticity of the brain have the tremendous capacity," Jensen explained, "to reduce or eliminate the negativity of the traumas children sometimes bring with them to class."

It's also rather convenient that these intervention strategies are not just neuroplastically beneficial to trauma-affected students; they can be used with all students to reduce or regulate negative classroom emotions and self-handicapping behaviors in order to achieve academic success more efficiently.

Most educators have never been trained in identifying and reacting strategically to traumatized students. Yet, they are somehow expected to manage classrooms in which well over half of the students may have experienced traumatic stress, oftentimes chronically, and are penalized if they can't.[3] Consequently, they still rely overwhelmingly on obsolete systems of threat and punishment.

Not every troublesome or irresponsible student has experienced trauma, but too many of them have. Unfortunately, childhood trauma is often tough to accurately identify as the catalyst for disruptive or self-defeating behavior. Many of our

---

[3] As we wrote it, this sentence triggered our memory of a quote we often use from Richard Carlson's *Don't Sweat the Small Stuff*: "One of the mistakes many of us make is that we feel sorry for ourselves, or for others, thinking that life should be fair, or that someday it will be. It's not and it won't. When we make this mistake we tend to spend a lot of time wallowing and/or complaining about what's wrong with life. 'It's not fair,' we complain, not realizing that, perhaps, it was never intended to be." So, what we're trying to say here is...

students have experienced adverse childhood experiences, but that doesn't automatically mean that they been traumatized by them. Children react differently to the negative experiences of their lives outside school. Children (adolescents included) are typically reluctant or unable to discuss these experiences, which exaggerates the difficulty in identifying and reacting strategically to traumatized students.

Accordingly, perhaps the most strategic thing we could do is expose ourselves to, practice, and become relatively proficient in as many trauma-informed tactics as possible (which is essentially the purpose of this book). This way, we'll be better equipped to support all students, inclusive of those who have experienced trauma and trauma-based maladaptive neuroplasticity.

While it may sound naïve, futile, and even clichéd, the most trauma-informed strategy there is is establishing and maintaining positive educator-student relationships with *all* of our students, even the difficult (and potentially traumatized) ones that most days you really don't feel like having a positive relationship with. And while this may also sound like a fairly simple strategy, these relationships, in order to be effective and actually strategic, must feature certain characteristics (e.g., unconditional positive regard, trust, intentional avoidance of trauma triggers) that could be overlooked if not made explicit.

Demonstrating *unconditional positive regard* for each student is arguably the most fundamental commitment an educator must make when establishing trauma-informed relationships with them. Alex Shevrin described unconditional positive regard as "the belief that every student is worthy of care and that worth is not contingent on anything—not compliance with rules, not good behavior, not academic success." This is specifically relevant in educator relationships with students impacted by trauma.

Childhood trauma (typically perpetrated by an adult the student initially expected would absolutely care about them) negatively biases how these students perceive potential relationships with adults. It diminishes their capacity to be naturally trusting, which causes them to doubt the reliability and test the commitment of the adult and the relationship instinctively. These students expect to be disappointed by (and disappointing to) any adult in their lives (*you* included). Oftentimes, their defiant, disruptive, defeatist, or disrespectful behavior is more indicative of them intuitively investigating the conditions of your positive regard than pure delinquency.

In reaction to past trauma, their survival-oriented brain[4] has been distinctly reformed and repurposed to now automatically *anticipate* future trauma (regardless of accuracy or evidence) as a defense mechanism. This chronic hypervigilance causes children who have experienced trauma to tend to be distrustful or suspicious of adults—especially those in a position to potentially harm them physically or psychologically (e.g., devalue or reject them)— because they expect adults to be untrustworthy and inevitably hurt them.

"When our students," particularly those who have experienced trauma, "know we'll care about them no matter what" and we won't suddenly stop caring because of something they say or do, they'll be more apt to risk establishing and maintaining a relationship with us.

Stephen Joseph emphasized that "unconditional positive regard is not about liking" all (or any) of our students or excusing their negative behaviors or being a perfect teacher that somehow never responds nonstrategically to those behaviors. It's about seeing all of our students, not as the sum total of their current behaviors, but as human beings "with agency to choose how to

---

[4]   The human brain is principally designed to support human survival by ensuring that we, as humans, make danger a priority. Rudolf Gregurek alleged that "the human brain's most important task is to keep the individual alive." Our brain, described David Amodio, is a "survival machine." It was created to feel, perceive, process, retain, and react to information from our circumstances for one preeminent purpose: physical and psychological survival. In other words, the human brain is survival-oriented.

7

respond to their situation and that no matter how dangerous or dysfunctional they seem to be, they are doing their best."

We don't totally agree with the "doing their best" part of Joseph's explanation. It's arguably more accurate to apply Jensen's aforementioned logic that some of our students are "faced daily with overwhelming challenges" that other students "never have to confront, and their brains have adapted to suboptimal conditions in ways that undermine good school performance."

We as educators must appreciate the observable fact that their brains have maladapted (i.e., changed negatively) in order to simply survive their circumstances, most of which are uncontrollable and many of which are potentially traumatic. And then use this appreciation to reinforce our "belief that every student is worthy of care and that worth is not contingent on anything," especially in those moments when certain (possibly traumatized) students appear to us (and perhaps themselves as well) to be unsalvageable, beyond remedy, gone, incorrigible, incurable, irreclaimable, irredeemable, irreversible, irrevocable, lost, or past hope.

It's in those moments of consistent disgust coupled with overwhelmedness, fatigue, frustration, disappointment, joylessness, hopelessness, anxiety, anger, neglect, shame, disrespect, and helplessness that our *positive regard* realizes and then attempts to somehow conceal, deny, or rationalize its conditionality.

Oftentimes, educators focus more on attempting to control students than practicing compassion, and it seems as if that tendency has strong roots in our actual lack of unconditional positive regard for all of our students. Control of behavior becomes a priority when our expectation of student misbehavior is greater than our academic (performance) expectations. This trend is particularly prevalent in high-poverty, high-minority classrooms where the stigma associated with Blackness[5] and poverty[6] appears to exaggerate the perceived disruptiveness (i.e., negative behavior) of Black and/or poor students collectively.

By prioritizing this need to control (do what I want) we concurrently prioritize the conditions for our positive regard (if you do what I want, then I will care about you). If we limit or withdraw our care for certain students when they do those things we do not approve of, then our students gradually learn that they are only cared about when they do the "right" things. This is *conditional* positive regard.

So, what happens to students impacted by childhood trauma who (because of trauma-based maladaptive neuroplasticity) tend to struggle with regulating negative emotions and impulsivity as well as overcoming their overreliance on self-handicapping academic behaviors. These students, noted Jensen, rarely consciously "choose to behave differently, but they are faced daily with

---

[5] "The (mostly) unspoken belief about black students," explained Fenwick, "is tied to broader perceptions about black people." These broader perceptions are typically based on the stigma of being Black promoted throughout the sociocultural experience of virtually all Americans. "Teachers' expectations of students are formed not by who the students are as individuals but, instead," explained Robert Tauber, "by the mere fact that the students are seen to be part of a larger group. The expectations, then, that are held for the larger group extend to the individual students."

What makes so many teachers implicitly anticipate that most, rather than some, Black students are disruptive and deficient is simply the fact that these students *are Black* and stigmatically, being Black is associated with so many negative behavioral traits (i.e., lazy, hostile, irresponsible, rude, unruly, etc.) along with the long-held assumption that Black people are genetically intellectually inferior.

[6] As a result of the stigma of poverty, poor people are generally expected to be lazy, trifling, incompetent, repugnant, and dangerous. Their poverty, especially when intergenerational, is perceived as somehow their fault, a consequence of their own inherent inadequacy rather than systemic joblessness in contemporary America.

overwhelming challenges that [untraumatized] children never have to confront, and their brains have adapted to suboptimal conditions in ways that undermine good school performance."

Regrettably, "brains are designed to reflect the environments they're in"—inclusive of negative race or poverty-based experiences they may endure repeatedly—"not to 'automatically' rise above them."   Accordingly, with regard to students experiencing complex trauma, they're "different" but only "because their brains are different" as a result of trauma-based maladaptive neuroplasticity.

Accordingly, they are inclined to disproportionately engage in disruptive classroom antics, apathy, absenteeism, noncompliance, incompetence, excuses, vulgarity, and misplaced aggression (all things that we as educators do not want them to do). Considering the conditionality of our positive regard, how will they ever be worthy of being cared for (by us)?

If the teachers they see almost every day continue to (presumably) unwittingly retraumatize them with adult relationships based on conditional positive regard, how will *these* students ever overcome the chronic hypervigilance that causes children who have experienced trauma to be distrustful or suspicious of adults?

And what if it's most of their teachers reacting this trauma-ignorant way throughout their young lives; what could be the cumulative effect on their humanity?   What would be their motivation to do better (as opposed to becoming emotionally nihilistic) if it's only a matter of time and circumstance till they do something wrong and fail to meet our conditions of positive regard (and are devalued or rejected again)?

Joseph wrote that "human beings have an innate urge towards socially constructive behavior which is always present and always functioning at some level." We have a natural desire to engage in positive (as opposed to disruptive or self-defeating) behavior. Moreover, we have "a need for self-determination; and the more a person's need for self-determination is respected, the more likely their innate urge to be socially constructive will take hold."

Perhaps you're already beginning to see the dilemma. Students impacted by childhood trauma tend to struggle with regulating negative emotions and impulsivity as well as overcoming their overreliance on self-handicapping academic behaviors; thus, they disproportionately demonstrate negative classroom behaviors relative to their untraumatized counterparts.

The more these students demonstrate negative classroom behaviors, especially if they are Black and/or poor and these behaviors are perceptually exaggerated due to the stigma of being Black or poor, the more their teachers and administrators will attempt to control their behavior (i.e., imposed outer-determined behavior). The less their behavior is truly self-determined, the more their otherwise natural motivation to demonstrate positive behavior will be diminished.

As this natural motivation to do right lessens, the more acceptable it becomes to the student to *not* regulate negative emotions and impulsivity or overcome their overreliance on self-handicapping academic behaviors. And the more unlikely these students (and their teachers) are to establish and maintain positive relationships with adults (these students) that could have triggered positive neuroplasticity.

Demonstrating unconditional positive regard requires what appears to be an atypical degree of informed intentionality, psychological effort, and emotional discipline. Regrettably, the capacity to intuitively and authentically demonstrate unconditional positive regard for each student is arguably the most uncommon trait of contemporary educators, especially those damned to teach in high-minority, high-poverty schools. This is perhaps made even more difficult when students are reflexively perceived as *others* (i.e., members of a social outgroup) relative to their mostly White, middle-class teachers.

Bernard Whitley and Mary Kite wrote at length about humans have a "tendency to see the world in two categories, *us* and *them*,

11

and this tendency perpetuates stereotypic judgment." Psychologically, we tend to create "categories on the basis of characteristics that a particular set of people appear to have in common. Through this process, people place others (and themselves) into categories called social groups. Once these social groups are created, people develop beliefs about the members of those groups. They then use these beliefs to guide their future interactions with individual social group members."

Race is one of the "primary categories for organizing information about other people, making [it] likely to be the first piece of information people take in about another." Being "racist" has nothing to do with it. Race is also a basic social category, "or a category for which a wealth of information is available in memory. When people know a person's basic category membership, such as race, they use that information to draw conclusions about the person's traits, social roles, and physical characteristics." Black people in America are probably associated with more negative social information (i.e., racial stereotypes and stigma) than any social group; we are the most highly stigmatized group largely because of our unique history in this country.[7]

Additionally, according to Marimba Ani, the human mind is designed "to think in terms of dichotomies or 'splits.'" First "the dichotomy is presented, then the process of valuation occurs in

---

[7] Glenn Loury described how an "awareness of the racial 'otherness' of blacks is embedded in the social consciousness of the American nation owing to the historical fact of slavery and its aftermath. This inherited stigma even today exerts an inhibiting effect on the extent to which African-Americans can realize their full human potential. Fundamental to the processes of race-making in the United States have been the institution of chattel slavery and the associated rituals and customs that supported the master-slave hierarchy and dishonored the slave. In the experience of the United States, slavery was a thoroughly racial institution. Therefore, the social meaning of race that emerged in American political culture was closely connected with the dishonorable status of enslavement."

12

which the self is valued and the other is devalued. The self is considered 'good,' positive, superior; the other is considered 'bad,' negative, inferior."

Kristin Anderson agreed that this human tendency to categorize "goes beyond overgeneralization to affect positive and negative judgments and treatment. Social psychologists use the term valence to describe positive or negative directional valuing. Ideas about ingroups and outgroups are valenced, meaning there is a tendency for people to view and treat members of their ingroup favorably, and members of the outgroup unfavorably." In other words, it's much easier to demonstrate unconditional positive regard to members of your ingroup and basically required that positive regard for members of an outgroup *feature* conditions— especially a highly stigmatized racial outgroup.

Being trauma-informed—especially in a high-poverty, high-minority school—initially requires the extraordinary ability and inclination to transcend all of this *human stuff*. It's probably important to note that demonstrating unconditional (as opposed to conditional) positive regard requires lots of practice and self-reflection. John Teasdale described it as "a habit, it's something the more one does, the more likely one is to be in that mode with less and less effort."

Relationship building, especially with students potentially impacted by trauma, can be extremely difficult and occasionally seem pointless. The relationships we establish with our potentially traumatized students may become the most influential of all our students with regard to setting the overall tone of our classrooms. How strategically we react to the impulsive and self-handicapping behaviors of our potentially traumatized students has the most influence on these relationships. The more strategic our reaction, the more likely our potentially traumatized students will trust that we are not a threat and it's safe to allow us to teach them. The more student-teacher trust is established, the less our potentially traumatized students will have to rely on impulsive and self-defeating behaviors to avoid the lingering threat of emotional retraumatization in the classroom. The fewer of these behaviors we have to address, the more effort we can then exert on highly quality instruction and ultimately greater student achievement.

Stephen Covey concluded that "relationship trust is all about consistent behavior. People judge us on behavior not intent." Student-educator trust largely comes from the innate consistency of demonstrating unconditional positive regard. Most teachers assume their students automatically trust them because they're teachers. Most students—particularly those in high-poverty, high-minority schools—do not trust their teachers simply because they're teachers because most of their teachers have not demonstrated unconditional positive regard for them.

"Contrary to what most people believe, trust is not some soft, illusive quality that you either have or you don't; rather, trust is a pragmatic, tangible, actionable asset that you can create—much faster than you probably think possible. And doing so will have a huge impact, both in the quality of our relationships and in the results we're able to achieve."

We cannot afford to wait on our students, especially those potentially impacted by trauma, to initiate trust-building; to do so is generally outside of their psychological capacity. However, as we work to establish positive relationships with and provide high quality instruction to all of our students, explicitly building student-educator trust must be our top priority daily. "Trust changes everything. So, let's commit to working on building trust."

We are among the adults our students spend most of their daily lives with; consequently, much of their capacity to respond constructively to childhood trauma is based on our actions (even when we are in no way responsible for that trauma). Our relationships with those students who have experienced childhood trauma can create the foundation required for reversing much of the trauma-based maladaptive neuroplasticity they have most likely endured. This can all sound somewhat intimidating at first, but there are several relatively straightforward things we can do

14

every day in our classrooms to develop student-teacher trust, demonstrate unconditional positive regard, and plant the trauma-informed seeds of positive neuroplasticity.

Establish reliable structure, routines, protocols, and predictability in your classroom. All students (and their brains) benefit from positive consistency, but none more than those otherwise living in chaos and chronic adversity. And, to quote Lincoln Chafee, "trust is built with consistency."

Resist the instinctive need to immediately and overemotionally react to negative student behavior, particularly when you can feel your or their anger, frustration, or perception of threat escalating. Pause, be silent for a moment, and create the space between stimulus and response to engage your empathy, foster emotional de-escalation, and find the most productive response.

Listen strategically to all of your students. Richard Carlson described strategic listening as "being content to listen to the *entire* thought of someone rather than waiting impatiently for your chance to respond." Not listening strategically "encourages us to criticize points of views, overreact, misinterpret meaning, impute false motives, and form opinions, all before [the student] is even finished speaking." By talking too much, by being counter-argumentative, by being hypercritical, by not reducing distractions, by interrupting students or finishing their sentences—we instigate conflict and create the perceived conditions of our positive regard.

Use humor routinely to inject positive emotional experiences like happiness, enthusiasm, enjoyment, and calm into your classroom. When our students see us laugh and smile more, mirror neurons in their brain encourage them to laugh and smile more too and better regulate negative emotional experiences like criticism, conflict, disappointment, and distrust. And research confirms that happier students are more academically motivated, resilient, and successful. Tanner Wallace et al. explained that "teachers' use of humor played a role in how students perceived being known by that teacher. To effectively use humor required shared experience

15

and a certain level of nuanced knowledge of that student's personal history. In turn, a kind of reciprocity in attention and respect developed between students and their teachers."

With regard to their behavior, offer your students, especially those showing signs of possible traumatization, choices and consequences as opposed to arguing and confrontation. With students our goal should always be to stay calm and avoid or de-escalate confrontation; too much confrontation can ruin the student-teacher relationship. I totally understand that this is easier said than done, but being a teacher *is* hard and, at least in America, *totally optional*.

Publicized, preset choices and consequences, when used properly, enable educators to drastically reduce the need for arguing and confrontation. If you (student) do this negative thing, then this is the consequence (or perhaps a choice of consequences). Bam! Thanks to logic, there's no real emotional urgency needed in that process. More importantly, there's no need for a power struggle, which usually evolves into arguing and confrontation. This is even more effective when the consequences are something you as the classroom teacher have created and have control over, versus sending them to the Principal's office (which can be perceived as conditional rejection).

As trauma-informed educators, we initially need to determine whether or not and why we care about our all of our students and actually aspire to do so unconditionally. "One of the cruelest things you can do to another person," Douglas Coupland advised, "is pretend you care about them more than you really do." And typically, students can tell rather quickly and accurately if we do care about them unconditionally or don't.

It's difficult, if not impossible, to constantly hide the conditionality of our positive regard; even when you're not conscious of it your students may very well be. Several studies, acknowledged Rhona Weinstein, "provide evidence of leakage—that is, contradictory messages expressed across different channels of communication. For example, teachers were less able to

16

control" this conditionality "in facial expression or bodily position than in speech." In other words, you may *say* you care, but you don't *act* like you care.

Beyond not being trauma-informed, maybe you just don't (or somehow can't) care *like this*, and teaching in an environment where trauma-impacted students (and their disproportionately disruptive classroom antics, apathy, absenteeism, noncompliance, incompetence, excuses, vulgarity, and misplaced aggression) are more the norm than exceptional is not something you'll ever be successful with. It doesn't automatically make you a bad person or even a bad teacher. To quote Cookie from *Empire*, "the streets aren't made for everybody. That's why they made sidewalks."

Most teachers don't know (or haven't yet accepted) that many negative student classroom behaviors, especially those rooted in trauma, are actually preceded by (sometimes unintentionally) negative teacher behaviors. We're not excusing negative student behavior by attempting to shift blame to teachers. In fact, we have consistently communicated that the *only person whose behavior you can control is you.*

However, when it comes to teaching students possibly impacted by childhood trauma, it's noteworthy that oftentimes it's a negative teacher behavior or reaction, regardless of intentionality, that triggers a traumatic stress response within the student's brain. And then the stress response prompts the student's inability to regulate (i.e., not act out) negative emotions, impulsivity, and/or self-handicapping academic behaviors.

Much of the negative student behaviors we experience—particularly in high-poverty, high-minority classrooms—are actually consequences of chronic, yet unintentional, *retraumatization* in the classroom. Retraumatization, according to Karen Zgoda et al., is a "conscious or unconscious reminder of past trauma that results in a re-experiencing of the initial trauma event. It can be triggered by a situation, an attitude or expression, or by certain environments that replicate the dynamics (loss of

17

power/control/safety) of the original trauma"—this is referred to as a trauma trigger.

A trauma trigger can pretty much be anything (a person, place, perception, behavior, situation) that somehow reminds you, knowingly or unknowingly, of a previous traumatic experience or how you felt or psychoemotionally reacted during the experience. These triggers can be terribly difficult to identify, anticipate, avoid, or control.

Teacher behaviors that typically become trauma triggers for students who have experienced trauma (especially when these behaviors are chronic) include being emotionally inconsistent or unstable; having poor classroom management; executing rough transitions between activities; humiliating students; yelling at, scolding, threatening, or arguing with students; being sarcastic; disregarding (i.e., overtly lowering their academic expectations of) disengaged, disruptive, or low-performing students; demonstrating bias or favoritism; lecturing too much (i.e., using whole-class lectures and discussions as their dominant teaching method); being overly strict and restrictive (i.e., having too many unnecessary classroom rules); engaging in racial microaggressions; and being hasty in referring students to office/administration (and as an administrator, being hasty in suspending or expelling students).

Accordingly, being a trauma-informed teacher requires a daily, reflection-based commitment to not commit/continue these behaviors.

There are moments when a student's behavioral reaction to a classroom situation or your own behavior seems especially inexplicable or inappropriate. In these moments, it is most likely that the situation or behavior has somehow triggered a traumatic stress response in that (apparently traumatized) student's brain. In these moments, it is critical that you (as probably the only trauma-informed person in the room) 1) identify the behavior for what it

18

possibly is (and sometimes it won't necessarily be retraumatization) and 2) strategically encourage de-triggering[8].

When a student is retraumatized, the current experience (i.e., trauma trigger) provokes them to automatically feel or psychoemotionally react similarly to how they did during the past traumatic experience (or experiences). They are experiencing in that moment (in your classroom of all places!) some kind of perceived threat to their psychological (and sometimes even physical) well-being. And this perceived threat is accompanied by an abrupt inability to regulate their negative emotions (e.g., feeling overwhelmed, afraid, angry, rejected, helpless, trapped) or think or behave rationally.

All thought and behavior in that moment—even if disruptive or self-handicapping—is psychological (and sometimes even physical) survival-oriented. The student's primary concern in that moment (as opposed to learning from or listening to you) is somehow stopping the negative emotions associated with the perceived threat without having adequate access to those parts of the human brain that typically stop negative emotions. The reply then becomes using other/more negative emotions (and emotional behavior) to try to stop the negative emotions currently being experienced, which is akin to attempting to extinguish a housefire by using other/more fire.

At this point these students need to be de-triggered. Unfortunately, at this point most teachers (and remember, most teachers are not trauma-informed) respond with being emotionally inconsistent or unstable; having poor classroom management; executing rough transitions between activities; humiliating students; yelling at, scolding, threatening, or arguing with students; being sarcastic; disregarding (i.e., overtly lowering their academic expectations of) disengaged, disruptive, or low-performing

---

[8] De-triggering basically involves 1) identifying your trauma triggers (which assumes you are already cognizant of having experienced trauma) and 2) consciously deciding (and learning how) not to succumb to these triggers. Neither step is particularly easy, by the way.

students; demonstrating bias or favoritism; lecturing too much (i.e., using whole-class lectures and discussions as their dominant teaching method); being overly strict and restrictive (i.e., having too many unnecessary classroom rules); engaging in racial microaggressions; and being hasty in referring students to office/administration.

Yes, this means that students who are experiencing retraumatization in our classrooms are oftentimes responded to with additional trauma triggers; instead of de-triggering, *we* are retriggering. And yes, this is a bad thing (and a worse thing if we continue doing it after being informed).

Ideally, we'd like to prevent retraumatization in our classrooms. While complete prevention is outside of our control, *reducing* retraumatization in our classrooms is something we can control mostly by decreasing those aforementioned teacher behaviors that typically become trauma triggers for students who have experienced trauma—especially when you consider that most of the negative student behavior we're reacting to is more so annoying (to us) than malignant.[9]

The first teacher behavior we'd recommend regulating a lot more intentionally is yelling at, scolding, threatening, or arguing with our students. The level of hostility with which a teacher verbally reacts to negative (but not life threatening) student behavior should never be so egregious that it becomes a trauma trigger; yet somehow this has become the norm, particularly in high-poverty, high-minority classrooms.

Children who have not had the opportunity to form secure attachments with the adults in their lives because of past trauma may perceive all adults as potential psychological (and perhaps even physical) threats. This perception automatically jeopardizes the functionality of their student-teacher relationships; a student

---

[9] Not sweating the small stuff helps us to reduce those teacher behaviors that may be trauma triggers for our students. "Learning to stop sweating the small stuff," explained Carlson, "involves deciding what things to engage in and what things to ignore."

won't/can't learn from you very efficiently once their brain prioritizes reacting to you as a threat (because their stress response is now active). Traumatized children can be uniquely "sensitive to nonverbal cues, such as tone of voice, volume, posturing, and facial expressions," explained Elizabeth Keller-Dupree, particularly cues indicative of confrontation. So, once you repeatedly display cues that are (or can be perceived as) unnecessarily confrontational (e.g., yelling at, scolding, threatening, or arguing with), these cues can confirm (to them) that you are what they thought you were: just another threat.

Accordingly, as clarified by Susan Cole et al., "many traumatized children adopt behavioral coping mechanisms that can frustrate educators and evoke exasperated reprisals, reactions that both strengthen expectations of confrontation and danger and reinforce a negative self-image." However, their (potential or actual) trauma doesn't somehow excuse the hostility with which we communicate; if anything, it should motivate us (as educators aspiring to successfully educate all students) to not behave in a way that we become seen as just another adult threat to not trust and act out towards or avoid.

Requiring trauma-informed educators to stop (or at least strategically minimize) yelling at, scolding, threatening, or arguing with students should not insinuate a request to lower their academic and behavioral expectations of potentially traumatized students. It *is* a request to change how we communicate and enforce higher expectations for all students. For many children who have experienced trauma and trauma-based maladaptive neuroplasticity, a teacher yelling at, scolding, threatening, or arguing with them merely escalates or perpetuates their negative classroom behaviors, so why would we continue to not practice a less confrontational style of responding? Teacher ignorance (of trauma-based student behavior and trauma-informed responses), indifference, inflexibility, incompetence, implicit bias, ill intentions (we're assuming that was not a rhetorical question—and we really enjoy alliteration).

21

Being trauma-informed means actively changing how we perceive students and react to their negative classroom behaviors. It's means, explained Bloom, learning and adopting strategies that enable us to shift the basis of our response from "what is wrong with you?" to "what happened to you and how can I help?" when addressing disruptive or self-handicapping student behaviors. Making this shift can "be very hard for teachers, some of whom have been exposed to trauma themselves," noted Pamela Cantor.

Educators who practice deescalating their reactions to negative student behavior enable student-educator relationships based on trust and unconditional positive regard to evolve organically. Things like an overly aggressive tone of voice and communication habits can really jeopardize these relationships, especially with students who have experienced trauma.

Most people (educators included) are simply unaware of the impact of their speaking tonality and communication habits, so being strategic when them is never considered as a necessary aspect of their profession. For educators, there is a very fine line between sounding authoritative and being perceived as too aggressive; and our ignorance of this line is a liability with regard to being trauma-informed.

Many educators (us included for many years) wrongly believe their aggressiveness is simply suggestive of being firm with and having higher expectations for their students, but being (perceived as) too aggressive can actually be counterproductive when it comes to potentially traumatized students. Teacher aggression is oftentimes perceived by these students as anger, and anger, especially from an adult authority figure, can be a trauma trigger— and not just for whoever the aggression is directed to. A teacher using an overly aggressive tone with another student in the same classroom or hallway may trigger a traumatic stress response in a traumatized student, but it will probably seem as if the latter student is being irrationally disruptive or disengaged (as opposed to responding to trauma that we unnecessarily triggered).

When dealing with negative behavior from potentially traumatized students, it is better to speak like Ramone from the Pixar movie *Cars* rides, "low and slow." (Ramone was the candy painted 1951 Impala low-rider, by the way.) Lower volume, slower rate of speech, shorter sentences, exaggerated pauses between sentences, fewer questions, more conversational than preachy, more matter-of-fact than emotional tone, and minimal body movements are all preferable communication habits. It's not rocket science, but like all good habits, it takes intentionality, self-discipline, and lots of practice to communicate like this instinctively.

The commonness of students in classrooms across this country experiencing trauma is greater than most of us would ever comfortably imagine, especially in high-poverty, high-minority schools. But just what is *trauma*?

The Early Trauma Treatment Network described trauma as "any exceptional or chronic experience"—sexual abuse or assault; physical abuse or assault; emotional abuse; neglect; witnessing domestic violence; parental separation or divorce; homelessness or residential instability; being a victim or witness to community or school violence; forced displacement; physical or emotional parental abandonment; having household members who are mentally ill, suicidal, drug addicted, or incarcerated; serious accident or illness; being bullied; being a victim or witness to natural or man-caused disasters; exposure to acts of war, terrorism, or political violence; or the death of a peer or a family member— "in which powerful and dangerous stimuli overwhelm an individual's capacity to regulate their emotions" and "ability to cope with what they have experienced."

When any of these aforementioned experiences occur in one's childhood and overwhelms the child's "capacity to regulate their emotions" and "ability to cope with what they have experienced," it is referred to as childhood trauma.

Trauma is not necessarily "an event in itself," noted Lenore Terr, "but is instead the reaction to extremely stressful life circumstances." Trauma is a distinct type of stress. Traumatic experiences are "extraordinary, not because they occur rarely, but rather because they overwhelm the ordinary human adaptations to life," wrote Judith Herman. "They confront human beings with the extremities of helplessness and terror."

SAMHSA defines trauma as "an event, series of events, or set of circumstances that is experienced by an individual as physically or emotionally harmful or threatening and that has lasting adverse effects on the individual's physical, social, emotional, or spiritual well-being."

"At one time, trauma was considered an abnormal experience," but now we know that "trauma exposure is common in the United States" regardless of race or socioeconomic status.

"Trauma is defined less by the event itself," described Beth Glanville, "and more by the effects of the event on the individual." Trauma is a state of extreme psychological "arousal, either sudden or sustained, in which the adaptive coping mechanism of a person shuts down," explained M. Gerard Fromm. "The essence of trauma," according to Bessel van der Kolk, is that "it is overwhelming, unbelievable, and unbearable."

Trauma can be an overwhelmingly stressful experience that forever changes a child's natural belief that the world is just and safe and *their* world is controllable. The experience can be isolated (i.e., acute trauma), ongoing, or cumulative. For far too many Black children in America, particularly those living in intergenerational poverty, trauma is an underlying, chronic part of their daily lives because for them race (or racial stigma) and poverty—at a minimum—function as *complex* traumatic stressors. Race and poverty *are* (at least among) the situations they believe they have no control over that makes them feel constantly like the world is unfair and unsafe simply *because* they are Black and poor.

SAMHSA defines complex trauma as experiencing "repeated instances of the same type of trauma over a period of time" or experiencing multiple types of traumatic stressors. The experiences that cause complex trauma are usually psychologically as opposed to physically threatening; hence, their increased capacity to be recurring. Conversely, *acute* trauma can result from a single or isolated experience, an experience that is typically somehow physically life-threatening.

A psychological threat, according to Kennon Sheldon and Tim Kasser, causes "people to feel unsafe or anxious and can occur through a variety of means. For example, threats to self-esteem, social inclusion, people's sense of order and control, and people's survival or sense of continuity, while all distinct types of threats, have at base a commonality: the individual feels a sense of insecurity regarding impending trouble, danger, or harm."

Complex trauma involves recurring, prolonged, or cumulative exposure to trauma-inducing situations and experiences along with "the impact of this exposure on immediate and long-term outcomes," specifically trauma-based maladaptive neuroplasticity, "emotional dysregulation, and a lack of appropriate coping mechanisms, which in turn can increase the risk of further traumatic experiences."

Whenever we refer to trauma throughout this book, we're typically referring to complex trauma.

"Every traumatic experience is different," noted Cole et al., and even in comparable experiences, trauma (i.e., triggering the traumatic stress response) is not inevitable. Most of us have experienced some potentially traumatic situation or event as children (i.e., adverse childhood experiences), but were not necessarily *traumatized* by the experience. We may have felt emotionally overwhelmed in the moment by the experience, but we had access at some point to the internal and external resources to cope with and recover from the experience.

Being traumatized implies that the trauma-inducing experience was somehow able to instigate distinct, negative (or maladaptive), and enduring changes in a child's psychological capacity to regulate their emotional reactions (i.e., traumatic stress response) to highly stressful situations or events subsequently.

Complex trauma, because it involves the repetitive or chronic triggering of the traumatic stress response, is more likely to ultimately cause such a change than an isolated traumatic event (i.e., acute trauma).

In addition to being *omnipresent* complex (i.e., ongoing) traumatic stressors themselves, race (i.e., being Black in America) and intergenerational poverty (as opposed to situational poverty) also increases a child's vulnerability to complex trauma by naturally limiting their access to resources to cope with and recover from other, co-occurring traumatic experiences (e.g., rape, physical or emotional abuse, witnessing domestic or community violence). Consequently, nearly all Black or intergenerationally poor students are probably already to some degree impacted by trauma-based maladaptive neuroplasticity.

Students impacted by childhood trauma (because of trauma-based maladaptive neuroplasticity) tend to struggle with regulating negative emotions and impulsivity as well as overcoming their overreliance on self-handicapping academic behaviors. Accordingly, they disproportionately demonstrate negative classroom behaviors relative to their untraumatized counterparts.

Neuroimaging has confirmed that being traumatized in any way can structurally and functionally change the brain of the traumatized. "The organ being plastic," observed Philip Perry, "trauma fundamentally changes how the brain operates." However, complex trauma, because it is both emotionally overwhelming and ongoing, triggers the most neuroplasticity. The nonadult brain is especially neuroplastic and susceptible to traumatic stressors, so when a child or adolescent experiences unaddressed complex trauma (along with inadvertent retraumatization at school), trauma-based maladaptive neuroplasticity is highly probable.

According to Sethanne Howard and Mark Crandall, "if the trauma is severe, prolonged, or life threatening, sometimes the brain cannot quite heal the trauma, and there are long-term changes in the brain."

Traumatic stress is defined by the American Academy of Experts in Traumatic Stress as the "emotional, cognitive, behavioral, physiological experience of individuals who are exposed to, or who witness, events that overwhelm their coping and problem-solving abilities." Whenever traumatic stress is "prolonged, extreme, or repetitive, the neuron pathways in the amygdala lose their 'elasticity' or ability to recover." As a result, "the brain keeps sensing danger, sending out stress response signals," and releasing certain neurotransmitters and hormones such as cortisol. When neural structures and pathways are chronically awash with these brain chemicals and hormones, these neural structures and pathways can be significantly changed structurally or functionally.

Chronic traumatic stress can instigate lasting changes in certain brain areas, particularly the amygdala, hippocampus, and prefrontal cortex. Kimberley Shilson acknowledged that "psychological trauma impacts such brain areas as the amygdala (involved in emotion management) and the hippocampus (involved in memory and memory consolidation). If trauma occurs repeatedly or over a prolonged period, cortisol (a hormone released during times of stress) is released too much, subsequently activating the amygdala and causing even more cortisol to be released."

An almond-shaped neural structure centrally located in the medial anterior temporal lobe, the amygdala (which is actually Greek for "almond") processes external stimuli and reflexively determines an emotional significance and response to that stimuli (particularly when deemed threatening), which is then sent out to other regions of the brain. The amygdala is directly associated with learned emotional responses (e.g., fear, anger, affection, disgust) and is *proportionately plastic*, which means chronic overactivation of neurons in the amygdala enlarges and hypersensitizes the amygdala (by strengthening its internal and outbound neural circuitry) which causes excessive, conditioned

27

emotional reactions to recurrent (and potentially threatening) stimuli.

In other words, the more we repeatedly (over)react emotionally to life circumstances, the more likely we are to (over)react equally emotionally to those same (or similar) life circumstances in the future because of changes to our amygdala. These reactions can become adaptive or maladaptive, more likely the latter as reacting emotionally subdues rational thought and authentic problem solving.

Constant cortisol saturation significantly changes neural structures like the hippocampus and prefrontal cortex (PFC), both of which are gradually reduced in size and activity as cortisol annihilates hippocampus and PFC neurons via prolonged overactivation. Conversely, continuous cortisol production increases the size and activity of the amygdala. According to research by Christopher Pittenger and Ronald Duman, chronic traumatic stress "enhances synaptic plasticity and the function of amygdala neurons, an effect quite distinct from the atrophy it induces in the hippocampus and PFC. This could both result from and contribute to overactivation of neuronal circuits that control fear, anxiety, and emotion."

The now hyperactive and hypertrophied amygdala promotes persistent states of hypervigilance and heightened emotional reactivity, even our stress response is exacerbated. The hypervigilant amygdala is constantly activating the stress response, and every activation makes a future activation much more likely (as it becomes patterned neuronal activity).

Chronic traumatic stress strengthens the neural pathway between the amygdala and hippocampus and weakens the neural pathway between the hippocampus and prefrontal cortex. Consequently, our fight or flight response to perceived traumatic threats (or traumatic reminders) is drastically quickened because our ability to moderate this response is linked to the functional efficiency of the hippocampus and prefrontal cortex, both of which are neuronally atrophied by continuous cortisol saturation. In other words, an exaggerated traumatic stress response is a consequence of the brain changes brought about by experiencing chronic traumatic stress.

Most of us are familiar with the term PTSD, or post-traumatic stress disorder. PTSD typically manifests in people who have experienced (or witnessed) a single traumatic event, especially one that was physically life-threatening (e.g., combat, car accident, natural disaster, rape, interpersonal violence).

Fewer people are familiar with *Complex* Post-Traumatic Stress Disorder (or C-PTSD), which is a distinct psychological reaction to multiple, recurring, or prolonged, (typically) severe traumatic experiences typically occurring in childhood. These experiences, which are usually more psychologically than physically threatening, include parental neglect or abandonment; emotional, physical, or sexual abuse; as well as witnessing or experiencing community, domestic, or war-related violence.

The brain of a child or adolescent experiencing chronic traumatization is more vulnerable to C-PTSD (and associated maladaptive neuroplasticity) primarily because the sense of uncontrollability attached to the traumatic experiences can be more overwhelming to nonadults naturally not as proficient or confident in their capacity to control external circumstances (e.g., to stop the traumatic experience) or their internal response to those circumstances.

This sense of uncontrollability can ultimately trigger a greater, more incessant traumatic stress response (and trauma-based maladaptive neuroplasticity) than the traumatic experiences themselves.

Exposure to the traumatic stress of uncontrollability causes an accelerated loss of PFC size and function and increase in amygdala size and function relative to "normal" traumatic stress. According to Avis Hains et al., "when we feel stressed and out of control, high levels of norepinephrine and dopamine release rapidly weaken PFC, while strengthening more primitive emotional responses and habits mediated by the amygdala."

Chronic exposure to the stress of uncontrollability induces greater "loss of PFC pyramidal cell spines and atrophy of dendrites...PFC gray matter decreases and PFC connectivity" weakens quickly. "This can save our lives when we are in danger and rapid, reflexive responding is needed, but can be detrimental when more thoughtful solutions are needed," such as those associated with a child's "capacity to regulate their emotions" and "ability to cope with what they have experienced."

A greater sense of sustained controllability increases the prefrontal cortex's ability to regulate and calm the amygdala, specifically as it relates to our perception of traumatic experiences. Uncontrollability, particularly when persistent, decreases that ability and, consequently, makes the amygdala far more active than necessary. More cortisol is released, eventually leading to prolonged cortisol saturation in certain brain areas.

Constant cortisol saturation, as aforementioned, significantly changes neural structures like the hippocampus and prefrontal cortex (PFC), both of which are gradually reduced in size and activity as cortisol annihilates hippocampus and PFC neurons via prolonged overactivation. Conversely, continuous cortisol production increases the size and activity of the amygdala. The now hyperactive and hypertrophied amygdala promotes persistent states of hypervigilance and heightened emotional reactivity, even our traumatic stress response is exacerbated. The hypervigilant amygdala is constantly activating the traumatic stress response, and every activation makes a future activation (e.g., retraumatization in the classroom) much more likely (as it becomes patterned neuronal activity).

The nonadult brain is already exponentially more neuroplastic than the adult brain, which biologically makes it more susceptible to C-PTSD. Further aggravating a child/adolescent's unique vulnerability to C-PTSD (and associated maladaptive neuroplasticity) is their natural tendency to compensate for relatively immature trauma coping skills via overreliance on self-blame.

It's not uncommon, according to Michelle Warren, for a child/adolescent to "attribute blame or ineffectiveness to themselves when they have been helpless participants" in repetitive traumatic circumstances or experiences. Faced with the aggravated stress of uncontrollability, children/adolescents are oftentimes limited to one of the most immature, narcissistic reasoning we have: *it's my fault*. Self-blame is a common yet damaging way we exert some sense of controllability over being traumatized.

Children/adolescents usually don't yet possess the ability to separate *themselves* from the unconscionable actions of their traumatizer (oftentimes a presumably trustworthy authority figure). Self-blame makes this even more difficult. Complex trauma experienced in childhood can then become a featured aspect of their personal self-concept; they *become* the trauma, even if only unconsciously. However, becoming the trauma, even if only unconsciously, triggers a desperate need to somehow become something (or someone) else.

Our self-concept—how we think about, evaluate, and perceive ourselves—can ultimately be devalued (i.e., negatively biased) as a result of experiencing complex trauma in our youth. Our self-concept, as described by Na'im Akbar, "is the way that we see ourselves. It is related to whether we see ourselves negatively or positively, usually based upon the information we have about ourselves and how others respond to us." This information usually comes from external sources like parents, teachers, peers, the media, people from other social groups, and our sociocultural environment.

How these sources respond to us largely informs "what we feel about who we are and what we do with what we are." The dilemma (and enduring damage to our self-concept) then comes when trauma hijacks the reliability of these external sources, especially when the trauma is instigated by one of the sources. Our experiences with trauma begin to convince us that "what we feel about who we are" should primarily be based on how our

31

traumatizers have responded to us, which is grossly negatively. We also tend to anticipate "future traumatizers" responding to us similarly and overreact accordingly (e.g., retraumatization in the classroom).

Our psychological reaction to complex childhood trauma oftentimes includes exceptionally devaluing our self-concept. Done unconsciously, this devaluation is intended to *defend* our self-concept from the traumatic stress of self-blame by "attributing exaggerated negative qualities to self," explained Randall Wickham and Janet West. In other words, whatever childhood trauma we've experienced is our fault because we somehow don't possess enough of whatever positive qualities would have prevented the trauma. A devalued self-concept is a distinct consequence of C-PTSD (as opposed to PTSD) whenever the devaluation is associated with complex trauma.

The traumatized child concludes that there is something deeply wrong with him or her and this profound flaw makes them in some way responsible for the trauma. Accordingly, they inevitably "think, feel, and act in ways that demonstrate the devaluation of themselves," explained Rita Hardiman and Bailey Jackson. Moreover, self-blame and, subsequently, self-devaluation delays the traumatized child in appreciating the lingering need to adequately cope with or truly overcome past traumatic experiences or regulate negative emotions and impulsivity in their present. The stress of their complex childhood trauma is converted into the stress of self-devaluation, with the latter being a much easier stress to disregard.

Complex trauma-based self-devaluation is particularly problematic (and maladaptively neuroplastic) for Black and/or intergenerationally poor children/adolescents who are already subjected socioculturally to stigma-based devaluation. Blackness (i.e., being Black) and intergenerational poverty are still profoundly stigmatized in America. Possessing either of these particular traits oftentimes comes with a persistent feeling of somehow being flawed and inadequate, or to quote Marilyn

32

Sorenson, "of *being* something wrong." This feeling can become so fixed and normal that we lose awareness of its existence and stigmatic origins.

Carol Miller and Cheryl Kaiser confirmed that not only can "stigma be a source of chronic stress for stigmatized people," it can ultimately become a complex traumatic stressor specifically because stigma is highly uncontrollable[10] and experienced as a "repeated instance of the same type of trauma over a period of time" or in addition to other types of traumatic stressors. Complex trauma involves recurring, prolonged, or cumulative exposure to trauma-inducing situations; stigma can certainly be such a situation.

Any type of chronic stress, particularly complex traumatic stress, can maladaptively change the human brain. Accordingly, stigma (especially prolonged stigma such as racial stigma) may trigger maladaptive neuroplasticity among stigmatized. Racial stigma-related stress can literally change the brain of African-American students, especially those from high-poverty backgrounds who must concurrently cope with chronic poverty related-stress and the accompanying neuroplasticity. Coupling this with the stress of "traditional" complex trauma (e.g., parental

---

[10] As noted by Gregory Herek, "stigma is not inherent in a particular trait or membership in a particular group; rather, society collectively identifies particular characteristics or groups, and assigns negative meaning and value to some of them, thereby 'constructing' stigma."

For instance, racial stigma, explained Robin Lenhardt, "like race itself—is ultimately a social construct. This means that the norms and rules about which categories of individuals will be valued or devalued are defined by society, even by the government, but not by nature. There is, after all, nothing inherently wrong with having dark skin or being a racial minority in society. Such a status does not itself lead to mistreatment or discrimination. An attribute that stigmatizes one type of possessor can confirm the usualness of another, and therefore is neither creditable nor discreditable as a thing in itself. An attribute becomes disfavored only because of the social information it carries."

neglect or abandonment; emotional, physical, or sexual abuse) only exacerbates these changes.

"Expressions of old-fashioned blatant prejudice may create different stressors than modern or subtle forms of prejudice. Some stigmatized people have expressed the view that it is easier to cope with blatant prejudice than it is to cope with subtle prejudice. At least they know where they stand with blatant prejudice, whereas it may be very difficult to identify what is going on when a person is subtly prejudiced or ambivalent about the stigmatized person. This can leave the stigmatized person with considerable ambiguity about what precisely is happening in a situation."

Even so, "the core feature of stigma is that a stigmatized person has an attribute that conveys a devalued social identity within a particular context. Compared to other types of stressors, stigma may be especially stressful because it poses some unique demands on the individual. Although stigma is defined as a devalued social identity in a particular context, for many stigmatized people the context in which they are devalued is pervasive. People with physically obvious stigmas, such as members of devalued racial groups, face potential prejudice and discrimination across a broad range of social contexts. Some stigmatized attributes are so powerful in the reactions they engender that they are 'master status' attributes that become the core, identifying attribute of the person who possesses them. Thus, stigma can increase the quantity of stressors stigmatized individuals experience."

Furthermore, stigma is "linked to the individual's social identity. This feature of stigma can increase the potential for stress because unfair treatment or judgments can be triggered simply by group membership and thus have implications for collective as well as personal identity. Threats to collective identity are multifaceted. Seeing other group members suffer from unfairness due to stigma may result in vicarious stress responses. Other people's devaluation of the group may reduce the comfort and sense of belonging that group membership normally provides.

Stigmatized people also may be pressured to be 'a credit' to their group or to otherwise represent their group to the nonstigmatized world. These stressors arise precisely because stigmatized people have a devalued social identity."

Racial stigma remains a chronically negative sociopsychological experience responsible for a variety of aversive reactions from those subjected to it. Research shows that recurring experiences of racial stigma, either directly or vicariously, cause stigma, shame, anxiety, anger, aggression, apathy, inequality, injustice, illness, despair, docility, self-handicapping behavior, stereotypic behavior, learned helplessness, and, perhaps most impactfully, complex traumatic stress. "Because stigma conveys a devalued social identity within a particular context," explained Mark Hatzenbuehler et al., "it creates unique stressors."

The stigmatized cannot control being stigmatized; if they could, they'd instantly stop being stigmatized or possessing the stigma (e.g., stop being Black). "Society," explained Gregory Herek, "collectively identifies particular characteristics or groups, and assigns negative meaning and value to some of them, thereby 'constructing' stigma." Stigma isn't constructed organically, arbitrarily, or benignly. Whatever characteristics or social groups that a society decides to negatively value are selected because it "consequently disadvantages, devalues, and disempowers those who have it."

The uncontrollability of stigma enhances its capacity to function as a complex trauma. Adding uncontrollability to an ongoing, potentially traumatic experience can make it even more overwhelming, especially to nonadults naturally not as proficient or confident in their capacity to control external circumstances or their internal response to those circumstances. The more overwhelming the experience—with regard to our capacity to regulate our emotions and cope with what we have experienced— the more likely we will respond to the experience as complex trauma. Uncontrollability can ultimately trigger a greater, more incessant traumatic stress response (and trauma-based maladaptive neuroplasticity) than the traumatic experience itself.

Jennifer Heller described stigma as "a phenomenon that occurs when power is exercised by a dominant group through means of labeling and stereotyping those that are perceived to be different." Instigating stigma requires social power; consequently, the currently powerful tend to create stigma exclusively for their own benefit (i.e., to rationalize or sustain socioeconomic privilege). According to Richard Parker and Peter Aggleton, "stigma plays a key role in producing and reproducing relations of power and control. It causes some groups to be devalued and others to feel they are superior. Ultimately stigma is linked to the workings of social inequality."

African-Americans currently lack the opposing social power required to end the stigma of Blackness in America; hence, our continued vulnerability to racial stigma as a potential complex traumatic stressor and the neuroplasticity it may cause to the areas of the brain involved in the process of perceiving stigma.

Sabrina Zirkel wrote that "stigmatized individuals are certainly aware of the negative stereotypes held about them. For some, the awareness of these negative stereotypes becomes a defining feature of how they perceive the world, and they become highly sensitive to race-based rejection or develop a strong stigma consciousness. The awareness of stigma and the everyday experiences of it remain a stressful and exhausting aspect of life for the stigmatized."

"Situations that evoke negative stereotypes are stressful." And this is exactly what stigma repeatedly does, constantly create interpersonal and institutional situations that evoke negative stereotypes. Stigma creates a unique "anxiety with which the stigmatized individual approaches interactions in society," explained Ilan Meyer. Stigmatized people (students included) "may perceive, usually quite correctly, that whatever others profess, they do not really 'accept' him and are not ready to make contact with him on 'equal grounds'" (teachers included). Much of the stress of racial stigma comes from the continuous anticipation of adverse stigma-influenced circumstances in our future.

Bruce McEwen and Peter Gianaros acknowledged that "an important aspect of allostasis and allostatic load is the notion of anticipation. Here, anticipation implies psychological states such as apprehension, worry, and anxiety, as well as cognitive preparation for a forthcoming event. Anticipation arising from neural activity within the brain can drive the output of allostatic biomediators, and it is likely that states of prolonged anxiety and anticipation can result in allostatic load."

Allostasis is the process of attaining the relative internal stability (i.e., homeostasis) required for survival through physiological, behavioral, cognitive, emotional, and/or neuroplastic responses to external stressors. According to David Borsook et al., "the brain responds to potential and actual stressful events by activating hormonal and neural mediators and modifying behaviors to adapt. Such responses help maintain physiological stability (allostasis). When behavioral or physiological stressors are frequent and/or severe, allostatic responses can become dysregulated and maladaptive (allostatic load). Allostatic load may alter brain networks both functionally and structurally" (i.e., allostatic load causes neuroplasticity). As a result, "the brain's responses to continued/subsequent stressors are abnormal, and behavior and systemic physiology are altered in ways that can, in a vicious cycle, lead to further allostatic load."

Oftentimes a psychosocial stressor, in order to be sufficiently alleviated (and allostasis achieved), requires a coping response that is beyond what we are currently capable of generating. This is particularly true when the stressor is ambiguously negative, unpredictable, chronic, and uncontrollable; the stress it produces is actually aggravated. Whenever we're not capable of coping effectively with certain stressors and cannot accomplish allostasis, the consequence is a cumulative effect known as allostatic load. With allostatic load, instead of achieving relative internal stability, especially with regard to emotional regulation, overutilization of the stress response (and oversaturation of neural structures and circuitry by stress hormones) is normalized as patterned neuronal activity, which triggers neuroplasticity.

We are convinced that more often than not we are perceived and (pre)judged not as an individual but as a Black person, and that this perception and (pre)judgment will be biased by the racial stigma of being Black in America. Not only are we convinced, we are chronically fearful of it (this concept is known as stereotype threat). And because it (as a group practice) can come from any White person, we tend to anticipate it coming from *every* White person (as well as other Black people). This constant anticipation and accompanying vigilance becomes a cumulative stressor.

Vigilance is a common means of defensively coping with being stigmatized. Somehow most Black people in America seem to "learn to anticipate—indeed, expect—negative regard from members of the dominant culture," explained Meyer. "To ward off potential negative regard, discrimination, and violence [we] must maintain vigilance. The greater one's perceived stigma, the greater the need for vigilance in interactions with dominant group members. By definition such vigilance is chronic in that it is repeatedly and continually evoked in the everyday life" of the stigmatized, who must "be constantly on guard, alert, or mindful of the possibility that the other person is prejudiced."

Psychologically, stigma creates a "conflict between self-perceptions and others-perceptions" for the stigmatized. "As a result of this conflict, self-perception is likely to be at least somewhat unstable and vulnerable. Maintaining stability and coherence in self-concept is likely to require considerable energy and activity. This exertion of energy in maintaining one's self-concept is stressful, and would increase as perceptions of others' stigmatization increase" (as with age and cumulative stigma-influenced interpersonal and institutionalized experiences).

The mere existence of racial stigma makes us more apt to semiconsciously anticipate being stigmatized regardless of whether we actually are being stigmatized (or perceived stigmatically) at the moment. Anticipation becomes self-protective. Unfortunately, anticipating being stigmatized, even if only semiconsciously, also becomes in itself a source of chronic stress.

Once we anticipate or perceive a threatening situation (e.g., racial stigma) often enough, our hippocampus and amygdala begin to condition our brain to believe that the situation is inevitable and records/repeats the anticipation we felt about it. In other words, whenever we constantly perceive a situation as threatening and typically react with the traumatic stress response, our amygdala forms an association between the perception and anticipation. The next time we're confronted with the perception, we will reflexively recall the traumatic stress we repeatedly felt before and feel it again. We will automatically feel traumatic stress, and once we accept the stress (or simply refuse to not accept it), the neural association between the perception and this reaction is reinforced. And because this happens so quickly, we have very little conscious control over it.

Poverty in America can be a stigmatizing experience because, to quote Erving Goffman, it results in the possession of another socially defined "undesired differentness. Stigmatized persons possess an attribute," in this case *being poor*, "that is deeply discrediting and they are viewed as less than fully human because of it."

Poverty (i.e., being poor) as stigma is an "enduring condition, status, or attribute," according to Herek, "that is negatively valued by society, that fundamentally defines a person's social identity, and that consequently disadvantages and disempowers those who have it." However, "stigma is not inherent in a particular trait or membership in a particular group; rather, society collectively identifies particular characteristics or groups, and assigns negative meaning and value to some of them, thereby 'constructing' stigma."

In other words, being poor is not naturally defining, devaluing, or discrediting. Poverty didn't become a "negatively evaluated

39

difference" until privilege and wealth needed to be justified. Being poor has become negatively perceived because we have been socialized to associate poverty with personal inadequacy or lack of effort as opposed to a consequence of structural inequality and targeted joblessness. A negative meaning has been assigned to being poor in America, which somehow justifies structural inequality and targeted joblessness. Poverty as stigma allows us to believe that it is not capitalism's inherent inequity that is at fault (i.e., causing poverty), it's the indolence, incompetence, or indifference (or culturally inadequacy) of the poor. Poverty as stigma allows us to shift blame as an entire society and thwart social rebellion by creating, to cite Joe Pettit, "a hierarchical separation of human worth."

It's easier to see poverty stigmatically when the poverty is intergenerational. Intergenerational poverty can become perceptually associated with a specific group affiliation, since it (i.e., being poor) is a distinguishable, negative trait that can appear to be passed on from one generation to another in a particular social group (e.g., African-Americans). Because it *endures*, intergenerational poverty becomes perceived as an "enduring condition," which is a core requirement of stigma (as well as complex trauma).

As a result of stigma, there exists a "prevalence of erroneous negative beliefs about people in poverty," noted Declan Gaffney. Stigma, explained Megan Steinhardt, "allows one to make negative judgments based on the label a person is given rather than on any actual behavior." As a result of the stigma of poverty, poor people (students included) are generally expected to be lazy, trifling, incompetent, repugnant, and dangerous. Behaviors that confirm this expectation are acknowledged (and typically even exaggerated) and those that don't are discounted as exceptional. Their poverty, especially when intergenerational, is perceived as somehow their fault, a consequence of their own inherent inadequacy rather than structural inequality and targeted joblessness in contemporary America.

"The idea that individuals can escape poverty through hard work is a fundamental tenant of American society," explained Marianne Page et al., but "intergenerational mobility is lower in the United States than in any other developed country in the world." Nevertheless, the mere persistence of intergenerational poverty becomes false confirmation of the appropriateness of the stigma attached to it.

Despite the true, structural origins of intergenerational poverty in America (e.g., corporate automation, globalization, residential segregation, welfare dependency), it inevitably begins to *appear* that specific social groups simply cannot stop being poor because of their own inherent (as evidenced by its apparent inheritability) inadequacy. If these people *could* stop poverty they would have (since being poor sucks), so they must *cannot* (presumably because they are lazy, trifling, incompetent, repugnant, and dangerous). This fallacious but popular argument tends to trigger the internalization of inequality among the intergenerationally poor (especially when poverty as stigma is combined with another enduring stigma), who consequently develop a deeply ingrained feeling of shame, defectiveness, hopelessness, and helplessness (or uncontrollability).

Unfortunately, there is no minimum age requirement for this to occur, and students begin at an early age to internalize inequality as they tangibly and stigmatically experience intergenerational poverty. This experience oftentimes evolves into complex trauma as it overwhelms their "capacity to regulate their emotions" and "ability to cope with" what they are experiencing. Along with devaluing their self-concept and triggering maladaptive neuroplasticity, intergenerational poverty as complex trauma experienced in childhood or adolescence can grossly underdevelop these students' self-efficacy in general and academic self-efficacy in particular.

Diane Craft and Patricia Hogan described self-efficacy as "the conviction that one is or is not capable of successfully performing the behavior required to produce a certain outcome, which affects

41

whether or not a person will attempt a certain behavior and determines the effort expended and persistence levels." Whenever academic self-efficacy is underdeveloped, self-handicapping classroom behaviors tend to become commonplace as students become less and less likely to take responsibility for their quality of life as adults.

When students don't genuinely believe in their ability to achieve academically (or in the impact academic achievement will have on their life chances, i.e., its capacity to overcome structural inequality and the stigma of race or poverty), it's harder for them to resist quitting, acting out, being disruptive, or exerting only minimal effort. High academic self-efficacy is directly associated with increased academic motivation, persistence, and resistance to negative thinking with regard to the types of academically adverse circumstances[11] all too common to Black and poor students.

Complex Post-Traumatic Stress Disorder should be viewed less as a traditional disorder or disease and more as the consequence of maladaptive neuroplasticity triggered by the overuse (or chronic use) of the traumatic stress response. Doing so could limit the stigma attached to C-PTSD (or PTSD in general) as well as our general reluctance as educators to use it to better understand and respond to negative student behavior, especially the behavior of Black and poor students.

This reluctance seems to semiconsciously stem from exaggerated, stigma-based expectations of these students being

---

[11]   To include lower teacher quality; a less impactful curriculum; lower per pupil expenditures; lower (i.e., stigma-influenced) teacher expectations regarding their academic performance; less effective classroom management; an overreliance on exclusionary discipline; higher student-to-teacher ratios; less access to new books, computers, the Internet, and other resources that stimulate or improve student engagement; a school climate generally less conducive to learning; practically nonexistent (or negligible at best) parental engagement and trust in the academic process; and significant (yet otherwise preventable) knowledge gaps.

42

innately disruptive and uncontrollable as well as academic disinterested and deficient (and, consequently, much harder to teach) somehow *because* they are Black and/or poor[12]. They presume *most* (not just *some*) Black and poor students are disruptive and deficient. These expectations compromise our otherwise instinctive capacity to respond to these students with unconditional compassion and positive regard (perhaps out of fear of discovering stigma-contradicting circumstances or appearing to endorse excuses for the behavior), but responding to all students with unconditional compassion and positive regard is essential to truly being a trauma-informed educator.

It's undeniable that once a large percentage of Black and poor students populate a school, teaching and learning oftentimes (but not inevitably) becomes inundated by their disruptive classroom antics, apathy, absenteeism, noncompliance, incompetence, excuses, vulgarity, and misplaced aggression. Educators tend to assume implicitly that it's because the students are Black and poor (and the stigma associated with being Black or poor), but what if these are actually consequences of Black and poor students being disproportionately impacted by complex trauma (and unintentional retraumatization by their educators).

Being disproportionately impacted by complex trauma[13] and, consequently, trauma-based maladaptive neuroplasticity, these students are more likely to struggle with regulating negative emotions and impulsivity as well as overcoming their overreliance

---

[12] And the stigma attached to Blackness and poverty in America creates a general expectation that Black and poor people possess certain negative characteristics simply because they are Black and/or poor, to include being unintelligent, inadequate, indifferent, lazy, disrespectful, unaccountable, troublesome, and uncontrollable.

[13] Largely because they typically experience the common trauma associated with the tangible consequences as well as the stigma of being Black and/or poor in addition to other possible, co-occurring traumatic experiences (e.g., rape, physical or emotional abuse, witnessing domestic or community violence).

on self-handicapping academic behaviors. These students, according to Jensen, rarely consciously "choose to behave differently, but they are faced daily with overwhelming challenges that [untraumatized] children never have to confront, and their brains have adapted to suboptimal conditions in ways that undermine good school performance." Being trauma-informed means that you understand this as a possibility—if not, a probability—and you respond to all students strategically and positively.

In trauma-ignorant classrooms where Black and poor students regularly "fail to comply with their teacher's wishes and directives, quickly the students are constructed as problems—'at risk,' behavior problems, savages—and those constructions become self-fulfilling prophecies," noted Gloria Ladson-Billings. "Before long, the classroom is no longer a place where these students are taught and expected to learn. Rather, it becomes a place where bodies are managed and maintaining order becomes the primary task."

Teachers here typically "teach students who may or may not wish to be students. That means that their teaching must engage, cajole, convict, and perhaps even fool students into participation." This requires a great deal of effort, and commonly teachers come to find it easier to simply demonize or avoid these students then to exert that much effort.

Teaching Black and poor students is uniquely difficult because so much energy usually has to be expended in motivating so many of them to overcome their devalued self-concept, scaffolding impulsivity and emotional regulation, discouraging self-handicapping behaviors, and attempting to resolve their significant knowledge gaps[14] via strategic reteaching—assuming you're at

---

[14] A disparity in what content or skills a student should know based on a nationally comparable K-12 curriculum compared to what content or skills they actually know or demonstrate proficiency in as a result of learning opportunities, expectations, attitudes, and experiences. This disparity is largely the cumulative result of the lowered, probably stigma-based expectations of a student's previous educators.

44

least pretending to aspire to effectiveness. With these students, it's usually not enough to just present material to be learned, and then step back and let the magic happen. But that's not *because* they are Black or poor. It's probably because these students are disproportionately impacted by complex trauma and, consequently, trauma-based maladaptive neuroplasticity.

We certainly concur with the notion that it can be *discernably* difficult to teach Black and poor students. For one, *they are* oftentimes lower achieving academically; the achievement gap, regardless of its deepest-rooted causes, is *real*. Relative to members of other subgroups, Black and poor students tend to do and learn less, fail more, score lower, have lower grade point averages, drop out more frequently, and commonly become uncompetitive with regard to admission into college and the skilled labor market. The applicable numbers simply can't lie, at least not regarding the outcomes (causes, however, are generally more deceptive).

At this point we believe it's also worth noting Danielle Lavin-Loucks' argument that the "sheer presence of an achievement gap based on race, ethnicity, and socioeconomic status implies an unequal educational system. Predicated on race and class divisions, the achievement gap is part of a larger legacy that intertwines individual and family resources with school quality, social capital, and educational opportunity." It is the direct, yet grossly understated consequence of the "pervasive nature of school inequality, institutionalized racism," and residential segregation.

Not discounting the factual evidence of the achievement gap, but we see this gap as indicative of a series of unfortunate circumstances (e.g., higher quality teachers leaving or avoiding schools with higher percentages of Black and poor students) rather than confirmation of the inherent deficits and defects of Black and poor students (or Black and poor *people* for that matter). Even this evidence is more comparable than conclusive or stigma confirming.

It basically comes down to choosing a "what happened to them" as opposed to a "what's wrong with them" approach. The former requires patience, which, to quote Carlson, "involves seeing the innocence in others." There is very little patience or presumption of innocence usually demonstrated with regard to Black and poor students, who are quickly condemned by educators unable (or unwilling) to look beyond their current behavior "so that they can see the innocence in where the behavior is coming from." Yet, the closer you are to the behavior (i.e., classroom teachers), the harder it can be to see any "innocence in where the behavior is coming from" (e.g., complex trauma).

According to Chris Stewart, "the dominant school reform discourse believes black" and intergenerationally poor "students are broken. It is the one point of agreement between liberals and conservatives as they debate questions of how to address the 'problem.' When there is failure the problem is the kids themselves." The habitually outrageous classroom behaviors and obvious knowledge gaps, the actual deficits and defects of many (but certainly not *most*) Black and poor students can effectively confirm this notion, especially if you were already semiconsciously inclined to do so.

But at the same time, so many of these students *are* well-behaved, highly motivated, self-controlled, eager to learn, very ambitious, etc. Sure, they struggle sometimes as well and are possibly traumatized, but their capacity to overcome the struggle and trauma confirms that these "children are capable, brilliant, intelligent beings who are captives in a system that was not designed for them or with them in mind. Their potential far exceeds their conditions. The unsurpassable worth ascribed to them by God is cruelly diminished—daily, systemically, and possibly on purpose."

Students experiencing complex trauma, explained Ray Wolpow et al., are "often operating within the mode of 'survival in the moment.' Survival in the moment," even when the moment occurs during class, is governed by hyperactive, cortisol-saturated

46

"pathways in the brain that appraise threat, sacrifice context for speed of response, make decisions outside of consciousness, and mobilize the body for fight, flight, or freeze." Consequently, these students are remarkably more inclined to emotionally overreact to (be triggered by) a current action or circumstance that somehow reminds them of past or ongoing trauma as if it could become current trauma. As opposed to critical thought or constructive coping mechanisms, fear of not psychologically surviving in the moment is prioritized and responses like impulsivity, emotional dysregulation, and self-handicapping behaviors are normalized as supposed survival techniques.

Their brain, concluded Mary Flannery, "is changed by repeated traumatic experiences" and this chronic triggering (or retraumatization). "The result is a brain that has structurally adapted" for psychological "survival under the most stressful circumstances—but not for success in school."

Complex trauma "interferes with being fully present with a 'learning-ready' brain," explained Christopher Blodgett. Complex trauma can "impair the development of children's ability to regulate their emotions and to control impulsive behaviors," confirmed Cole et al. "Reactions can be triggered in hypervigilant children if they feel they are being provoked or if something reminds them of the trauma. An incident or remark that might seem minor to a nontraumatized child may be perceived as threatening by a traumatized child, who then responds in a seemingly disproportionate way. It is helpful for teachers to know what triggers might cause a traumatized child to become hyperaroused or to reexperience a traumatic event in the classroom."

Teachers and administration "may be able, through careful observation, to identify some of the child's triggers. Often, however, the help of a mental health expert is needed to be sure of what may be triggering a particular child."

To teach them effectively, educators have to deliberately develop unconditional positive regard for these students;

47

consciously accept that much of their defiant, disruptive, self-defeating, and indifferent behavior are oftentimes out of their control (i.e., unknown triggers, underdeveloped capacity to self-regulate); and consistently practice trauma-informed responses to the behavior. You have to develop an instinctive understanding that the behavior you're currently witnessing isn't necessarily indicative of the student's authentic attitude or altitude. It's possibly a consequence of a lot of concealed trauma and frustration mixed with *not a lot* of self-worth and confidence in ever being successful.

This doesn't mean, however, that teachers and school administrators can't hold these students accountable. Most of us initially and incorrectly associate being trauma-informed with lowering our academic and behavioral expectations of students apparently experiencing trauma. Knowing trauma (and trauma-based maladaptive neuroplasticity) is not an excuse for lower academic expectations or to not discipline negative student behavior. Being trauma-informed does not somehow mean that teachers and school administrators can't hold all of their students accountable. Holding a potentially (if not probably) traumatized student accountable is just more restorative and strategic as opposed to simply punitive and instructionally straightforward.

Experiencing ongoing or co-occurring childhood trauma repetitively triggers the traumatic stress response, which typically becomes a catalyst for maladaptive neuroplasticity. This phenomenon has relatively recently been labeled Complex Post-Traumatic Stress Disorder (or C-PTSD), with the neuroplasticity aspect either minimized or somehow excluded (in favor of emphasizing C-PTSD as a *psychological disorder* as opposed to the consequence of stress-related brain changes).

C-PTSD, suggested Eric Newhouse, is a "neuroplastic disorder par excellence" because when a child or adolescent with an otherwise normally functioning nervous system experiences recurring, prolonged, or cumulative exposure to trauma-inducing situations, the "brain is completely rewired by it."

48

As aforementioned, reframing our focus from C-PTSD as conventionally applied to *maladaptive neuroplasticity attributed to complex trauma* may increase educators' willingness to use it to better understand and respond to negative student behavior, especially the disproportionately criticized behavior of Black and poor students. This would be very similar to how Eric Jensen brilliantly used an emphasis on neuroplasticity to encourage teachers to "teach with poverty in mind." *Teaching with trauma in mind* essentially means becoming trauma-informed, or developing a specific proficiency with regard to how complex trauma can change a student's brain and how to strategically respond to these changes.

The past and present thoughts, observations, feelings, actions, and (over)reactions of every human being on this planet are all the result of neural activity occurring in our brain. Consisting of billions of connected neurons (or nerve cells) via neural pathways and neural structures, the human brain is a remarkably complicated entity capable of profound consistency as well as tremendous change.

Our brains are constantly changing and adapting to the circumstances of our lives, especially those that prove to be consistent or chronic. Our thoughts, observations, emotions, actions, and (over)reactions with regard to these circumstances deeply influence this change process, known as *neuroplasticity*, and those things that are most persistently thought of, observed, felt, acted out, and (over)reacted to create the strongest neural pathways and most altered neural structures.

The human brain is not at all static; it continually adapts and adjusts to pattern-repetitive thoughts, emotions, observations, actions, (over)reactions, and experiences. James Zull wrote that "the brain is molded and reshaped by the forces of life acting on it. Our wiring grows and develops depending on what we experience" directly or even vicariously. As a result of neuroplasticity, recurring thoughts, emotions, observations, actions,

49

(over)reactions, and experiences effectively become neurostructure.

The human brain is literally formed (and reformed) under the influence of external and internal stimuli on neural pathways, functions, and structures. Consider your brain as a vast series of continually forming circuits (or wires). Each circuit is a chain of aroused neurons. Neurons are the primary cells of the brain (the other type of brain cell are glial cells, which exist only to maintain neurons), each enclosed by branches (or dendrites) that send and receive electrochemical signals (i.e., information) from other neurons. Each neural circuit distinctively affects our cognitive, emotional, or behavioral responses to the circumstances of our lives. These circuits are created by our experiences, especially those experiences associated with stress. In fact, most of our neural circuits are formed either throughout our first three years of life or when we experience chronic stress.

Experience changes our brain by activating or overacting certain neurons or neural structures as well as altering neural circuitry. When we consistently or intensely experience something, the neurons in our brain associated with our action or reaction to that experience *fire* (i.e., are activated) repeatedly. When neurons fire repeatedly, they grow (or more specifically, their dendrites grow) and extend themselves out toward other neurons, eventually forming neural connections (or circuitry) via the connecting neurons' synapses. The new neural circuitry sends electrochemical signals back and forth over billions of connected neurons within specific areas or structures in our brain. Neural circuitry processes information and mediates human behavior.

Neuroplasticity, Rudolf Gregurek recognized, is a "precondition for any persisted behavioral change, behavior, cognition, and emotion." Neuroplasticity is possible because of the capacity of neurons to extend and create connections between brain regions and structures in order to facilitate efficient recall of past experiences and emotions along with reflexive instigation of a response.

Emotions are equally as influential as experiences in the altering of neural circuitry. The brain experiences emotion via the release of certain neurotransmitters (or brain chemicals) like adrenalin and dopamine as well as hormones such as cortisol. When neural structures and pathways are chronically awash with these brain chemicals and hormones, neural structures and pathways can be significantly changed structurally or functionally. We call all of this neuroplasticity, the ability of neural structures and pathways to change in response to a stressful or chronic experience or emotion. "Our brains," explained Jensen, "adapt (i.e., change) to *survive* our circumstances."

The commonness of students in classrooms across this country experiencing complex trauma and trauma-based maladaptive neuroplasticity is far greater than most of us would ever comfortably imagine. Most studies have concluded that 25-40% of all students have already been exposed to (and their brains changed by) some type of acute, compound, continuing, or co-occurring childhood trauma.

Although any student could experience complex trauma, those concurrently experiencing racial injustice, inequality, and stigma and/or intergenerational poverty are more vulnerable to trauma-based maladaptive neuroplasticity because of the sheer chronicity of their traumatic stressors. Just being Black or poor can conceivably be a *daily* stressor capable of prompting stimuli "powerful and dangerous" enough to "overwhelm an individual's capacity to regulate their emotions" and "ability to cope with what they have experienced." Coupling being Black or poor with other possible, co-occurring traumatic experiences (e.g., parental abandonment, sexual assault, physical or emotional abuse, witnessing domestic or community violence) exacerbates this chronicity.

Chronic (including co-occurring) traumatic experiences trigger chronic traumatic stress. Chronic traumatic stress prompts more neuroplasticity than acute traumatic stress because it causes a more continuous release of certain plasticity-inducing neurotransmitters

51

and hormones like cortisol. When neural structures and pathways are more awash with these brain chemicals and hormones, certain ones (e.g., the amygdala, hippocampus, and prefrontal cortex) are more significantly changed structurally and functionally.

Additionally, the more our brain responds to chronic traumatic stressors by repeatedly activating the traumatic stress response and releasing stress hormones (e.g., cortisol), the more of a stimulus-reinforcement association is established. These associations are patterned neuronal activity in which certain emotions (or even thoughts) are paired with specific external stimuli (or life circumstances) in order to increases the probability of a specific response (e.g., stress). Patterned neuronal activity changes the neural structure and functioning of the brain; thus, stimulus-reinforcement associations are in effect catalysts of neuroplasticity.

It's also worth noting that the more we employ the traumatic stress response, the more hyperactive the response itself (along with the neural structures and pathways associated with it, e.g., the amygdala) becomes until we find ourselves constantly hypervigilant, (semiconsciously and mostly inaccurately) perceiving potential threats to fight or flee ubiquitously.

Hence, success-oriented educators in schools that are high-poverty and/or have higher percentages of African-American students should be constantly mindful that these schools also have higher percentages of *probably traumatized* students (i.e., students most likely experiencing complex trauma and trauma-based maladaptive neuroplasticity at least as a consequence of race or poverty) than their more affluent and/or White counterparts.

Considering the traumatic impact of race and poverty, instead of the aforementioned 25-40%, in *these* schools we're possibly looking at closer to 80-90% of students presumably having already been exposed to (and their brains negatively changed by) complex trauma.

Regrettably, neither racial injustice, inequality, and stigma nor intergenerational poverty are readily accepted as complex traumatic stressors, even though they just as capable of prompting

52

recurrent stimuli "powerful and dangerous" enough to "overwhelm an individual's capacity to regulate their emotions" and "ability to cope with what they have experienced" as more acknowledged traumatic experiences (e.g., parental abandonment, sexual assault, physical or emotional abuse, witnessing domestic or community violence).

Race and poverty are highly prevalent traumatic stressors— logically—in schools that have higher percentages of Black and poor students. However, because race and poverty are not typically recognized by educators as traumatic stressors, trauma is not looked at as the most likely motivation for the common negative student behaviors experienced in such schools. Moreover, becoming more trauma-informed is not particularly valued by educators in schools that have higher percentages of Black and poor students as a means of becoming more effective in managing these negative student behaviors.

Although it's rarely ever admitted publicly or spoken aloud, it's constantly implied in subtle interpersonal interactions (e.g., racial microaggressions) and stubborn institutional inequities that "there are few advantages associated with being Black in America," noted Kathy Russell. Because of racism, observed James Baldwin, "being Black in America," even for a child, is "a terrible thing to be" and possibly even repetitively traumatic.

"Insufficient insight into the systemic nature of racism," wrote Philomena Essed, "fuels denial and the generic accusation that black people are oversensitive and resort too quickly to charging racism." Sufficient insight into the systemic nature of racism reveals why so few White people wish to be seen or see themselves as racist (or beneficiaries of racism) while, nevertheless, racism persists, factually and tenaciously.

Racism is a "coherent complex of oppression continuously present and systematically activated personally through encounters, vicariously through the experiences of other Blacks (or people of color), through the media and through the daily awareness of racial injustice in society."

53

Eduado Bonilla-Silva observed that "most whites insist that minorities (especially blacks) are the ones responsible for whatever 'race problem' we have in this country. They publicly denounce blacks for 'playing the race card,' for demanding the maintenance of unnecessary and divisive race-based programs, such as affirmative action, and for crying 'racism' whenever they are criticized by whites. Most whites believe that if blacks and other minorities would just stop thinking about the past, work hard, and complain less (particularly about racial discrimination), then Americans of all hues could 'all get along.' But regardless of whites' 'sincere fictions,' racial considerations shade almost everything in America."

For all intents and purposes, racism still operates as an "organizing principle of social relations in itself." Within systems of oppression such as racism, explained Rita Hardiman et al., racial differences are constructed and consistently "used as an indicator that demarcates those who will benefit from oppression and those who will be targeted by it. An individual will have more or less power, privilege, and access to resources within a system of oppression, depending on whether the group to which she or he is perceived to belong to."

Erin Winkler described how "factors in children's environments, and in our society as a whole, teach children that race is a social category of significance...children pick up on the ways in which whiteness is normalized and privileged in U.S. society. For very young children, this comes in the form of picture books, children's movies, television, and children's songs, which all include subtle messages that whiteness is preferable."

"Researchers have found that even very young children develop what psychologists call 'ingroup bias,' or favoritism towards the groups in which they are members. However, as children become more aware of societal norms that favor certain groups over others, they will often show a bias toward the socially privileged group. In a variety of studies, 'white children rarely exhibit anything other than a pro-white bias,' while children of color as young as five years old show evidence of being aware of, and negatively impacted by, stereotypes about their racial group."

Numerous scholars concur that race is a common source of complex trauma. Racism, noted Jennifer Crocker, "continues to place countless individuals in a position of hopeless discontent." Among Black people in America (children and adolescents included), acknowledged Alex L. Pieterse et al., "negative psychological responses to racism carry many features associated with trauma."

Ongoing exposure to *race-based traumatic stress* is a consistent consequence of simply being Black in America. "Race-based experiences," explained Robert Carter et al., "fall within the domain of traumatic experiences. Racism should be understood as an experience that can produce stress, and that in some cases, the stress can rise to the level of a traumatic stress reaction."

"Some racial and ethnic minority individuals may experience racial discrimination as a psychological trauma, as it may elicit a response comparable to posttraumatic stress." For the experience to be traumatic (i.e., trigger the traumatic stress response), it must somehow be "ambiguous, negative, unpredictable, and/or uncontrollable," which definitely describes most contemporary race-based experiences.

These experiences can also be severe or subtle, explicit or covert, "occur on an interpersonal level (microaggressions, verbal assaults, use of symbols or coded language)," "be the effect of structural or systemic acts," "occur on an institutional level, as an application of racial stereotypes or as encounters and assault(s)," or "occur through cultural racism." These experiences can become traumatic "when they have memorable impact or lasting effect or through cumulative or chronic exposure."

A race-based experience can be traumatic if it's a "violent event marked by sudden or extreme force from an external agent." However, the *violence* could "be psychological or emotional rather than physical. Extreme force could refer to the intensity of the emotional impact of the event. The external agent could be an act of racism, a race-based encounter," the tangible circumstances attributable to systemic racism, or the perpetrating racist(s). "The multiple and persistent ways in which racism affects marginalized populations can become traumatizing," noted Terrence Jordan.

"Racist acts today rarely include a stressor that involves the possibility of death, serious injury, or damage to physical integrity," confirmed Glenn Miller. Consequently, "race-based traumatic stress reaction does not fulfill the stressor criterion" for simple Post-Traumatic Stress Disorder (or PTSD), which requires the experience be perceived as physically life-threatening.

Racism may still function as a traumatic catalyst, according to Janet Helms et al., "even when there is no recent evidence of threat to life" and may operate as an "exacerbating stressor" to "commonly referenced traumatic situations" (e.g., emotional, sexual, or physical abuse; witnessing domestic violence; parental neglect or abandonment; homelessness or residential instability).

Racism may be "conceptualized as trauma because it is a form of victimization imposed and perpetuated by powerful others, which can produce post trauma-like symptoms (e.g., helplessness, fear)." Racism prompts recurring "race-based threats to one's emotional and psychological well-being," which can be "sudden or systemic, intentional or not, vague and ambiguous, direct and specific, or vicarious. Regardless of the form racism takes, racist incidents are, at minimum, a form of emotional abuse and, therefore, can be traumatic."

"Events experienced as negative, out of one's control, sudden, ambiguous, and repeated increase an individual's stress response," noted Carter et al. Accordingly, "these events deepen emotional pain and can lead to traumatic responses, including hypervigilance, avoidance or numbing and emotional distress." Experiences can be "traumatic because they are emotionally painful," explained Eve Carlson, or "because they involve the threat of emotional pain. In this case the negative valence is related to the psychological meaning of the event to the individual, not the physical consequences of the event." Racism consistently creates such

56

events and experiences for Black people in America, regardless of age, and should therefore be viewed as a *probable* traumatic stressor for Black people in America, students included.

Lillian Polanco-Roman et al. agreed that "racism is a potential source for traumatic stress." In fact, "racial discrimination may be better conceptualized as a race-based traumatic stressor rather than as a benign negative experience." Because "social situations in the United States are often tinged with race," explained Evangeline Wheeler et al., "Blacks in the Unites States are more likely to engage in cognitive appraisal of racism, and are thus more likely to feel stress."

What makes racism particularly traumatic for Black people in general—and Black youth in particular—is its inherent uncontrollability. A race-based experience, according to Carlson, may be traumatizing "if it is experienced as uncontrollable and sufficiently negative."

"The belief that one has some degree of control over events" (e.g., to stop race-based experiences), realized Carter et al., can "serve as a form of protection. Trauma is more likely in situations in which one believes that he or she is not able to control the highly negative event(s)."

As aforementioned, adding uncontrollability to an ongoing, potentially traumatic experience can make it even more overwhelming, especially to nonadults naturally not as proficient or confident in their capacity to control external circumstances or their internal response to those circumstances. The more overwhelming the experience—with regard to our capacity to regulate our emotions and cope with what we have experienced—the more likely we will respond to the experience as complex trauma. Uncontrollability can ultimately trigger a greater, more incessant traumatic stress response (and trauma-based maladaptive neuroplasticity) than the traumatic experience itself.

"There are many aspects of racism at its various levels (individual, institutional, and cultural) that render encounters and resulting manifestations as negative, uncontrollable, and sudden.

57

Yet, it is also true that, given the centuries of racist practices, some elements of racism can be considered predictable and constant but not in a way that permits a sense of control. Most forms of racism constitute assaults" on the subordinated outgroup member's sense of self (i.e., Black people's self-concept).

"While it may be known that racism exists in many areas of life in the United States, it is not possible to know when or how one may encounter specific racial incidents or what emotional or psychological impact the encounter will have. The inability to predict when or where such events may occur or to prevent them from occurring renders such events sudden and uncontrollable."

Black people must "determine on a regular basis if an event is related to one's race or not," which is a unique psychological burden that can result in traumatic stress. We are also limited in ways we can cope or adapt to race-based situation "in that many reactions may be met with social sanctions, and may thus create a greater degree of stress that could also push the stress to the levels of severity that produce trauma."

Being Black in America implies chronic (i.e., lifelong) traumatic exposure to race-based experiences[15]. "Because many aspects of racism can occur throughout one's life, severity may be a consequence of the cumulative effects of numerous events." These ongoing or recurring experiences, even when subtle or disguised, can (re)trigger race-based traumatic stress and ultimately evolve into complex PTSD (i.e., trauma-based maladaptive neuroplasticity). Some of the "symptoms that appear as a result of race-based traumatic stress include feelings of fear, anger, worthlessness, humiliation," and learned helplessness, noted Miller, which are consistent with C-PTSD.

---

[15]   Frederic Poag noted that because of racism "when you're white in America you're given the freedom to be an individual without the connotations and limitations of your race. In short, you're just a person, instead of a black person. That's an important distinction, and it's one that people who aren't white desperately want to get rid of."

"For African-Americans, racism is never a single act. It is expectable and persistent." W.E.B. DuBois wrote that racism, moreover, "doesn't mean that some act of terror or brutality" or blatant inequity "has to be committed against us every day. Racism simply means that such an act 'can always occur' any day—it means never being out of danger."

"Racial trauma may involve a negative, sudden, and uncontrollable experience or crisis," explained Kenneth Ponds. Or race-based traumatic stress may be triggered by "an ongoing psychological threat that produces feelings of fear, anxiety, depression, and helplessness. Much racial trauma is the result of what are called microaggressions, the everyday verbal or nonverbal slights, snubs, or insults (whether intentional or unintentional) which communicate hostile, derogatory, or negative messages to targeted persons."

As a primary trigger of race-based trauma, "microaggressions have a powerful impact upon the psychological well-being of the targeted group or person. Sadly, the most detrimental forms of microaggressions can be delivered by well-intentioned individuals who are unaware that they have engaged in harmful conduct toward members of a socially devalued group."

Derald Sue et al. described racial microaggressions as "brief and commonplace daily verbal, behavioral, or environmental slights, insults, indignities and denigrating messages, whether intentional or unintentional, that communicate hostile, derogatory, or negative racial slights and insults towards people of color. Studies support the fact that people of color frequently experience microaggressions, that they are a continuing reality in their day-to-day interactions" and result "in a negative racial climate and emotions of self-doubt, frustration, and isolation on the part of victims."

"Microaggressions are often unconsciously delivered in the form of subtle snubs or dismissive looks, gestures, and tones. These exchanges are so pervasive and automatic in daily interactions that they are often dismissed and glossed over as being innocent and innocuous." Regrettably, "almost all interracial encounters are prone to microaggressions." And "while hate crimes receive the most attention, the greatest damage to the life experiences of people of color is from racial microaggression."

Microaggressions create *insidious exposure*, which Carter et al. described as "both chronic and pervasive exposure to racism. Over time subjective experience of repetitive and cumulative exposure could be traumatically impactful. Such insidious exposure can reinforce assumptions that the world and life are unfair to people of particular races, that the dominant White race is at best unconcerned and at worst malevolent, and [Black] life has little positive worth and meaning;" such assumptions can become circumstantially traumatic.

"Because many aspects of racism can occur throughout one's life, severity may be a consequence of the cumulative effects of numerous events. For example, one seemingly innocuous or minor event could be the last straw in a series of accumulated racial incidents, causing a person to feel that he or she can no longer manage the stress and pain of encounters with racism. One may be stressed, but the level of stress may not reach the threshold for being traumatic until the trigger or last straw." In a similar study, Chalsa Loo et al. concurred that "the stressful effects of racism could be additive and that cumulative racism can be experienced as traumatic."

Students experiencing intergenerational poverty[16] live *lives* that are likely to be disproportionately ambiguous, negative, unpredictable, and uncontrollable (i.e., the four characteristic requirements for an experience to be considered traumatic). The omnipresent threat of poverty-related scarcity and susceptibility creates conditions ripe for chronic, braining-changing traumatic stress.

---

[16] As opposed to *situational poverty*, which does not persist into the next generation, is generally associated with a specific circumstance rather than systemic causes, and is somehow temporary.

We explained earlier that a stressor is basically anything (e.g., events, experiences, perceptions, or circumstances) that instigates stress (i.e., the stress response) once we are exposed to it. Stress is our brain's (over)reaction to any information from our external circumstances that somehow imply threat (e.g., threat of poverty-related scarcity). The stress response is also referred to as the "fight or flight" response because it effectively prepares us to either fight or flee from this implied threat.

The human brain, when faced with a real or imagined threat to survival, readies the human being to confront the threat or promptly get as far away (physically or psychologically) from the threat as possible. The fight or flight response is a reflexive reaction by the human brain to rapidly provide the body with those resources (e.g., increases in the release of certain hormones and neurotransmitters to enhance pro-survival functioning) required for either resisting or running from a threat. Whether this threat is psychological or physical, the same brain and body responses to threat occur, and because they have become automatic (or hardwired due to pass utility), the responses typically supersede critical thought or active choice for the sake of rapidity (and ensured survival).

Accordingly, a *traumatic* stressor is anything (e.g., events, experiences, perceptions, or circumstances) that communicates a threat so powerful and dangerous that it could overwhelm an "individual's capacity to regulate their emotions" and "ability to cope with what they have experienced" (i.e., physically or psychologically survive the experience). Trauma is not necessarily "an event in itself," noted Terr, "but is instead the reaction to extremely stressful life circumstances."

A traumatic stressor that is experienced as "repeated instances of the same type of trauma over a period of time" or as multiple types of traumatic stressors is considered a *complex* traumatic stressor. Complex trauma involves recurring, prolonged, or cumulative exposure to extremely stressful (i.e., trauma-inducing) situations and experiences along with "the impact of this exposure

61

on immediate and long-term outcomes," specifically trauma-based maladaptive neuroplasticity, "emotional dysregulation, and a lack of appropriate coping mechanisms, which in turn can increase the risk of further traumatic experiences."

The experiences that cause complex trauma are usually psychologically as opposed to physically threatening; hence, their increased capacity to be recurring. A psychological threat, according to Sheldon and Kasser, causes "people to feel unsafe or anxious and can occur through a variety of means. For example, threats to self-esteem, social inclusion, people's sense of order and control, and people's survival or sense of continuity, while all distinct types of threats, have at base a commonality: the individual feels a sense of insecurity regarding impending trouble, danger, or harm."

Intergenerational poverty, not just as stigma (as aforementioned) but the tangible and psychological consequences of intergenerational poverty, oftentimes becomes a complex traumatic stressor.

Intergenerational poverty, much like racism, "should be understood as an experience that can produce stress that in some cases can rise to the level of a traumatic stress reaction," explained Carter et al. It is typically experienced (beginning in childhood) as "repeated instances of the same type of trauma over a period of time," which qualifies as complex trauma. Intergenerational poverty also "significantly increases the probability of a child being exposed to a set of other stressors that can become traumatic," noted Carlos Pitillas, which makes poverty usually experienced in addition to other trauma (e.g., emotional, sexual, or physical abuse; witnessing domestic violence; parental neglect or abandonment; homelessness or residential instability).

When students experience intergenerational poverty, they grow up with the omnipresent psychological and tangible threat of scarcity and inequity. They grow up somehow realizing that relative to everyone else, explained Charles Sackrey, "poor people are typically able to enjoy fewer goods, do fewer things, and achieve fewer goals than all those above them in higher-income classes." This realization itself can become chronically traumatic.

To quote Melissa Phillips, poverty, particularly when intergenerational, is "a chronic fear of never having enough." This chronic fear may certainly become traumatic once coupled with the terrible implication that we apparently may not possess the competence or resources necessary to ever stop being poor (i.e., development of the poverty mindset).

The "trauma that's associated with never having enough," observed Jessica Trudeau, becomes a "perpetual trauma." For students experiencing intergenerational poverty, "every day, they're on high alert, so their brain is literally being trained to respond in that matter." Intergenerational poverty can be an overwhelmingly stressful experience that forever changes a child's natural belief that the world is just and safe and *their* world is controllable. These students, explained Jensen, are "faced daily with overwhelming challenges that affluent children never have to confront, and their brains have adapted to suboptimal conditions."

Their brains have maladapted (i.e., changed negatively) in order to simply survive their circumstances, most of which are uncontrollable and traumatic. Students experiencing intergenerational poverty are uniquely vulnerable to trauma-based maladaptive neuroplasticity and, consequently, tend to struggle with regulating negative emotions and impulsivity as well as overcoming their overreliance on self-handicapping academic behaviors.

Vanessa Jackson refers to intergenerational poverty as a potential "fiscal trauma," which she defined as an "intense emotional reaction, characterized by depression, anxiety/worry, a profound sense of shame, and a fear for survival in response to inadequate financial resources." The "life-threatening and shame-inducing experiences that result from inadequate income" could overwhelm an "individual's capacity to regulate their emotions" and "ability to cope with what they have experienced" and, consequently, become traumatic.

63

"When fiscal trauma intersects with racial oppression," added Lillian Drakeford, the chronic "stresses under which our students live" almost certainly become complex trauma.

Aggravating intergenerational poverty's capacity as a potentially traumatic experience is somehow understanding it not only as a negative personal experience, but as the ongoing, uncontrollable consequence of social exclusion and structural inequality.

In America, explained Douglas Massey, "labor markets did not arise out of neutral institutional matrices that guaranteed equal opportunity to all; instead, they were embedded in a social structure that was itself riddled with categorical inequalities based on race and class." America remains "the most unequal society in the developed world" largely because it was inherently created to be such a society.

Structural inequality is characteristic to capitalism, the socioeconomic system natural to this country. "Capitalism breeds poverty," concluded Sackrey, and "the poor are thus as inevitable a consequence of such a system as are the rich." Capitalism, "because it is competitive and aggressive, exacerbates whatever racial or other prejudices one may have to begin with. The competitive social order feeds upon the existence of losers." Consequently, "the capitalist order, as it has developed over time, has made it necessary to have an underclass."

Michael Parenti advised that "when trying to understand the persistence of poverty in modern capitalist nations, we should keep in mind that under capitalism private profit rather than collective need is the principal determinant of who gets what." And *how* they get what they get is based on certain systemic circumstances (e.g., an inherited wealth gap, targeted joblessness/labor obsolescence, corporate automation, corporate globalization, corporate suburbanization, residential segregation, imposed welfare dependency, educational inequity, White privilege) that conspire to sustain certain social groups' distinct vulnerability to intergenerational poverty. This group-based vulnerability typically trumps personal attributes and behavioral choices with regard to wealth accumulation, which intensifies its perceived uncontrollability.

Educational inequity is especially important (and uncontrollable) in the perpetuation of intergenerational poverty. To quote Sackrey, the currently affluent will "guarantee the entrance of their own children into the upper class by developing an educational system which stratifies the class structure by providing educational facilities and funds to students in direct proportion to the income of their parents."

And, "as a primary determinant in the perpetuation of poverty, there is also ample evidence to show that a poor person, especially if he is black, will receive fewer benefits from any given amount of education…If you are wealthy, chances are you will go to a suburban school, adequately financed, with the latest equipment, the best teachers, etc. The point is that the greater the resources your family has as you go to school, the greater the school system will add to your capacity to make income when you graduate."

Intergenerational poverty is only possible when there exists the possibility of intergenerational wealth, which is presumably the ultimate goal of capitalism (the true purpose of the profit motive). Most wealth is inherited (i.e., intergenerational). In fact, economists have estimated that almost 80% of a family's wealth derives from intergenerational transfers (i.e., inheritance).

The "configuration of both opportunities and barriers in workplaces, schools, and communities reinforce deeply entrenched racial dynamics in how wealth is accumulated," concluded Thomas Shapiro. "Due to the unearned advantages it transmits across generations, inheritance widens inequality." These advantages include the inevitability, according to Thomas Piketty, "that inheritance (of fortunes accumulated in the past) predominates over saving (wealth accumulated in the present). Wealth originating in the past automatically grows more rapidly, even without labor, than wealth stemming from work, which can be saved."

65

Wealth significantly determines an individual's life chances, yet African-Americans on average are five times less likely to inherit money than White Americans, White Americans' inheritances are ten times bigger, and, consequently, their familial wealth is about eight times that of ours. And while it's true that many among the contemporary affluent in America have amassed their impressive wealth via unprecedented opportunities in information technology, mass retail (including e-commerce), and finance, most of them (which excludes newly wealthy professional athletes and entertainers) still had direct access to significant intergenerational wealth for start-up capital. This reflects the sobering truth, to quote Shannon Moriarty, "that Americans have never had an equal opportunity to become wealthy."

"Wealth is a measure of cumulative advantage or disadvantage," explained Roderick Harrison. "The fact that black and Hispanic wealth is a fraction of white wealth also reflects a history of discrimination in which Whites have had more opportunities to accumulate wealth." Or as Dalton Conley recently phrased it, contemporary wealth reveals "the cumulative disadvantage of race for minorities or cumulative advantage of race for Whites," which originated during the American slavery era.

The uncontrollability of intergenerational poverty enhances its capacity to function as a complex trauma. Adding uncontrollability to an ongoing, potentially traumatic experience can make it even more overwhelming, especially to nonadults naturally not as proficient/confident in their capacity to control external circumstances or their internal response to those circumstances. The more overwhelming the experience—with regard to our capacity to regulate our emotions and cope with what we have experienced—the more likely we will respond to the experience as complex trauma. Uncontrollability can ultimately trigger a greater, more incessant traumatic stress response (and trauma-based maladaptive neuroplasticity) than the traumatic experience itself.

The chronic traumatic stress of intergenerational poverty (along with poverty as stigma), much like the chronic traumatic stress of racism and racial stigma, triggers continuous cortisol production which maladaptively increases the size and activity of the amygdala (while decreasing the size and activity of the hippocampus and prefrontal cortex). Consequently, negative emotional reactions (e.g., anxiety, anger, frustration, shame, hopelessness, helplessness) are easier to generate and harder to regulate.

Hence, success-oriented educators in schools that are high-poverty and/or have higher percentages of African-American students should be constantly mindful that these schools also have higher percentages of *probably traumatized* students (i.e., students most likely experiencing complex trauma and trauma-based maladaptive neuroplasticity at least as a consequence of race or poverty) than their more affluent and/or White counterparts.

Reconsidering the predictably traumatic impact of race and intergenerational poverty, instead of the 25-40% of potentially traumatized students in "normal" schools, in *these* schools we're possibly looking at closer to 80-90% of students presumably having already been exposed to (and their brains negatively changed by) complex trauma. So, success in these school *requires* educators to have some type of intentional, systemic focus on strategically supporting and *improving* all students' capacity to regulate their negative emotions and impulsivity, sustain positive relationships, and reduce their overreliance on self-handicapping behaviors as opposed to simply responding to them more negatively. This focus will concurrently strengthen all students' capacity to demonstrate higher levels of academic engagement, self-efficacy, self-resilience, and achievement as measured by state assessments.

Misery Won't Touch You Gentle[17]
Recognizing Chronic Traumatic Stress and Complex Trauma-based Maladaptive Neuroplasticity in Our Classrooms

"In short, the kids are different because their brains are different. Our neurons are designed by nature to reflect their environment, not to 'automatically' rise above it."

-Eric Jensen

"Trauma creates changes you don't choose."
-Michelle Rosenthall

"Children learn their experience; they don't necessarily learn what we intend them to."
-Norman Doidge

The Early Trauma Treatment Network described trauma as "any exceptional or chronic experience"—sexual abuse or assault; physical abuse or assault; emotional abuse; neglect; witnessing domestic violence; parental separation or divorce; homelessness or

---

[17] Excerpted from the following Edwidge Danticat quote from *The Farming of Bones*: "Misery won't touch you gentle. It always leaves its thumbprints on you; sometimes it leaves them for others to see, sometimes for nobody but you to know of."

residential instability; being a victim or witness to community or school violence; forced displacement; physical or emotional parental abandonment; having household members who are mentally ill, suicidal, drug addicted, or incarcerated; serious accident or illness; being bullied; being a victim or witness to natural or man-caused disasters; exposure to acts of war, terrorism, or political violence; the death of a peer or a family member; race-based experiences (e.g., racial injustice, microaggressions) or racial stigma; and intergenerational poverty—"in which powerful and dangerous stimuli overwhelm an individual's capacity to regulate their emotions" and "ability to cope with what they have experienced."

The "impact of trauma," acknowledged SAMHSA, "can be subtle, insidious, or outright destructive." But perhaps most significantly, according to Catherine Woodiwiss, "trauma permanently changes us." More specifically, the stress accompanying chronic (or complex) trauma can change our brain structurally and functionally. Most regrettably for students experiencing complex trauma[18], noted Michelle Rosenthall, "trauma creates changes you don't choose."

If it hasn't become glaringly obvious yet, we fully endorse psychoanalyst Norman Doidge's claim that "the human brain can change itself." In fact, according to Eric Jensen, our "brains are *designed* to change" because they possess plasticity. Thanks to neuroplasticity, the human brain can literally change and be (re)molded, intentionally and unwittingly, like plastic.

Neuroplasticity makes it possible for our brain's 100 billion interconnected neurons to continuously (re)create (or rewire)

---

[18] Reconsidering the predictably traumatic impact of race and intergenerational poverty introduced in the previous chapter, instead of the 25-40% of potentially traumatized students in "normal" schools, in schools that are high-poverty and/or have higher percentages of African-American students we're possibly looking at closer to 80-90% of students presumably having already been exposed to (and their brains negatively changed by) complex trauma.

neural pathways and modify neural structures throughout our lifetime. Neuroscientists are continually identifying just how malleable the human brain is as it enables us to perceive, plan, problem solve, self-handicap, rationalize, emote, act, interact, react, overreact, act out, remember, repress, rebel, internalize, fear, doubt, disrupt, and all things in between.

"*Neuroplasticity* is the quality that allows region-specific changes to occur in the brain as a result of experience." Regrettably, "brains are designed to reflect the environments they're in"—inclusive of negative race or poverty-based experiences they may endure repeatedly—"not to 'automatically' rise above them." Accordingly, with regard to students experiencing complex trauma, they're "different," but only "because their brains are different" as a result of trauma-based maladaptive neuroplasticity. Their brains have maladapted (i.e., changed negatively) to "suboptimal conditions" in order to simply survive their circumstances, most of which are uncontrollable.

"Nature has given us a brain that survives in a changing world by changing itself," noted Doidge. "Neuroplasticity is the property of the brain that enables it to change its own structure and functioning in response to activity and mental experience." Chronic experiences, especially those that are highly emotional (e.g., traumatic experiences), are most likely to produce brain changes that become quasi-permanent. Recurring thoughts, emotions, and experiences become patterned neuronal activity (i.e., neural circuitry) that can cause us to begin responding to the circumstances of our lives automatically based on these established neural activation patterns (i.e., brain changes).

The human brain, explained Arnulf Kolstad, "adjusts to the environment, the social situation, and to our psychological reactions. The brain develops new capacity as a result of our experience, our physical and mental activity, and how we cope with the situation. It stores what happens and creates new ways of thinking, feeling, and behaving. This quality of the brain is due to its 'plasticity,' or ability to develop and change. Physical and mental activity produces structural changes in the brain due to the brain plasticity in humans. The interconnections between neurons are changing all the time and brain structure is more like the software. This explains the importance of social and cultural influences since experiences are internalized and stored in the brain" as patterned neuronal activity.

"Neuropsychological research suggests that exposure to traumatic events and the consequent alterations in stress hormones cause alterations in the structure and functioning of the brain," confirmed Iris-Tatjana Kolassa and Thomas Elbert. The "amygdala, hippocampus, and prefrontal cortex (PFC) appear to be particularly involved in trauma-related neurocircuitry."

Complex traumatic experiences are most likely to change the human brain by repeatedly activating certain neurons or neural structures as well as altering neural circuitry, especially those experiences associated with chronic traumatic stress. "The organ being plastic," observed Philip Perry, "trauma fundamentally changes how the brain operates." However, complex trauma, because it is both emotionally overwhelming and ongoing, triggers the most neuroplasticity. The nonadult brain is especially neuroplastic and susceptible to traumatic stressors, so when a child or adolescent experiences unaddressed complex trauma, trauma-based neuroplasticity is highly probable.

Traumatic stress is defined by the American Academy of Experts in Traumatic Stress as the "emotional, cognitive, behavioral, physiological experience of individuals who are exposed to, or who witness, events that overwhelm their coping and problem-solving abilities." Because complex (as opposed to acute) traumatic stress is "prolonged, extreme, or repetitive, the neuron pathways in the amygdala tend to lose their 'elasticity' or ability to recover," explained Sethanne Howard and Mark Crandall.

As a result, "the brain keeps sensing danger, sending out stress response signals," and releasing certain neurotransmitters and hormones such as cortisol. When neural structures and pathways

71

are chronically awash with these brain chemicals and hormones, these neural structures and pathways can be significantly changed structurally or functionally.

Chronic traumatic stress can instigate lasting changes in certain brain areas, particularly the amygdala, hippocampus, and prefrontal cortex. Kimberley Shilson acknowledged that "psychological trauma impacts such brain areas as the amygdala (involved in emotion management) and the hippocampus (involved in memory and memory consolidation). If trauma occurs repeatedly or over a prolonged period," (i.e., complex trauma) then "cortisol (a hormone released during times of stress) is released too much, subsequently activating the amygdala and causing even more cortisol to be released."

"Our brains are wired to protect us from threat," noted Isaiah Pickens and Nicole Tschopp, "and no experience better represents threat than a traumatic event." A student's brain, once changed by complex trauma, tends to function in a constant state of fight or flight, anticipate or perceive threat (especially psychological threat) where there is none, and struggle to manage negative emotions in order to shift from the survival-oriented brain to the learning-ready brain when required. In reaction to past trauma, their survival-oriented brain has been distinctly reformed and repurposed to now automatically and primarily *anticipate* future trauma (regardless of accuracy or evidence and inclusive of the potentially traumatic psychological threat of anticipated inadequacy and failure) as a defense mechanism.

Most educators expect their students to "come into an academic environment ready to both learn and emotionally experience the enjoyment and excitement of discovery." However, according to Basha Krasnoff, brain changes caused by complex trauma "often block a child's ability to learn in the classroom. Children and adolescents are overwhelmed by the way their brains react to prolonged stress or trauma" by becoming "endlessly vigilant. Traumatized youth will do anything to survive—not because they want to but because they need to."

72

They stop taking enough of the positive academic risks (e.g., giving maximum effort, effectually responding to teacher checks for understanding, adequately studying for assessments, taking advantage of academic supports as needed) required for learning. Their brain tends to uniquely process these risks as most likely becoming shame-inducing experiences based on the perceived psychological threat of anticipated inadequacy and failure. Such experiences, like their previous or ongoing trauma, are expected to somehow overwhelm their "capacity to regulate their emotions" and "ability to cope with what they have experienced" and, consequently, become traumatic (or trauma triggers).

Perhaps most importantly, these students "stop relying on relationships to protect themselves," including those positive student-teacher relationships necessary for motivation, engagement, and resilience in learning. However, trauma-ignorant (and probably otherwise exhausted, demotivated) teachers may perceive this specific reaction as mere defiance, laziness, deficiency, or indifference, particularly for Black or poor students already negatively prejudged (typically semiconsciously) by stigma-based expectations.

As students experiencing complex trauma consistently withdraw from taking academic risks, relying on student-teacher relationships, and other pro-academic behaviors, the neural "circuitry for those activities begins to weaken," noted Doidge. This atrophy is the consequence of neuronal connections not being reinforced via repetition as well as neuroplasticity attributable to experiencing chronic traumatic stress (and continuous cortisol saturation of certain brain areas) in connection with their complex trauma.

They might try sporadically to be "good students," but "their brains will have trouble" with executing those unpracticed pro-academic behaviors, explained Eric Newhouse. Many of these students ultimately "develop something called learned non-use. Learned non-use is not a form of laziness; it is what the brain takes away from repeated efforts to do something, and finding it can't...it will ultimately quit trying" and deploy "its resources in other areas."

Doing so may then cause "harmful habits to become part of learned behavior" as the neural circuitry for some possibly anti-academic behavior begins to strengthen through repetition, especially if using them somehow consistently alleviates preexisting or predicted stress stemming from certain negative academic experiences. Self-handicapping academic behavior usually serve this exact function; it becomes a specific type of trauma-based self-defeating behavior[19].

---

[19]   Milton Cudney defined a self-defeating behavior as "an action or attitude that once worked to help an individual cope with a hurtful experience but that now works against the individual to keep him or her from responding to new moments of life in a healthy way. We develop self-defeating behaviors when...we adopt patterns of thought or action that reduce the pain and tension brought on by negative experiences. At a subconscious level, we associate these thoughts or actions with any subsequent reduction in our level of anxiety or discomfort. We form...a faulty conclusion that tells us that our self-defeating behaviors are appropriate responses to certain new moments of life."

"When an individual manages to cope successfully with a threat, the behavior that he or she has used to deal with it will become imprinted within that person's memory. Because the behavior has worked to eliminate a threat, it is stored within the individual's memory as an effective means of dealing with other threatening situations. Each time the individual encounters a situation that is ominous, he or she will react with the behavior that tamed the original threat."

A self-defeating behavior is "not truly born, however, until the individual connects in his or her mind the painful experiences and the behavior that eased the hurt or anxiety. When this connection is made within the person's unconscious mind, a *conclusion* is reached. This conclusion, in turn, becomes a basis for the way the individual chooses to behave in the future. The formula by which the person reaches this conclusion can be expressed as follows: experiences + behavior = conclusion. This formula—or, more accurately, the specific information that is substituted for each of its variables—is stored in the individual's memory. Each time the individual approaches a new moment of life, he or she unconsciously consults this formula and chooses a behavior that closely resembles the behavior used to reduce internal tension at the moment when the conclusion was reached. In this sense, the individual has become programmed for self-defeat. To try to protect him- or herself from further hurt or anxiety, the individual returns again and again to the behavior that was chosen when the conclusion was first formed."

"Experience plus behavior equals a conclusion. When we choose a self-defeating behavior in response to a painful experience, and when, subsequently, our internal tension is reduced, we are sending to our unconscious mind the conclusion that the behavior is a healthy and productive one. In this sense, the notion of lying to oneself takes on an added dimension. When we send a faulty conclusion to the unconscious component of our psychic subsystem, we are telling ourselves, essentially, that a behavior that hurts us is a good one. Instead of telling ourselves a truth that bears up to the test of reality, we are programming ourselves for defeat."

"Once a choice to behave in a self-defeating way has been delegated to the unconscious component of our psychic subsystem, the behavior starts to seem natural and automatic. The very fact that the choice is made on an unconscious level causes people to believe that the resulting pattern of self-defeat is simply part of their nature. Why do self-defeating conclusions exert such power over our behavior? The answer is simple: our self-defeating conclusions offer the promise of protection from hurt, pain, and anxiety. That this is a false promise does not matter, because within the individual's memory, both the self-defeating conclusions and the behavior it produces are completely logical."

"If a self-defeating conclusion, along with its promises of protection and control, remains stored within the unconscious component of our psychic subsystems, it will continue to exert its considerable power over the way we act and feel. In this dark region of the mind, the conclusions will survive as long as its own flawless logic remains in place. To eliminate a self-defeating behavior in this early stage of its development, therefore, we must retrieve from our unconscious minds the conclusion on which the behavior is based. Once we have brought the conclusion to the level at which we make conscious and informed choices, we can put it to the test of reality and reveal it for what it is: a distorted perception of how life works and of what must be done to avoid pain."

75

Self-handicapping occurs, according to Melissa Burkley, when students "select an obstacle to successful performance" (e.g., procrastination, giving low effort, not studying, quitting, being disruptive) thereby "enabling them to direct the cause of their poor performance away from their own incompetence and toward the obstacle. Thus, an individual *creates* an excuse in *anticipation* of an unsuccessful performance," and doing so reduces the stress associated with negative academic experiences such as the fear of failure (or actually failing).

Dina Nosenko et al. described self-handicapping as a "motivational strategy reflecting the efforts of the individual who anticipates failure in dealing with some significant goal-oriented activity to defend one's sensitive ego." Self-handicapping is a "maladaptive proactive coping strategy that opposes a set of other proactive coping strategies, all of which result in positive outcomes, such as preventive, strategic, anticipatory, and other forms of constructive proactive coping."

Self-handicapping academic behavior enables students to momentarily avoid both the effort required to control as well as responsibility for potential academic failures that could further degrade their fragile self-concept (possible consequence of complex trauma). The behavior typically sabotages their chances of academic success. It also encourages students to perpetuate semiconsciously the logical fallacy that it is somehow better (for one's self-concept) to self-handicap and then use the self-handicapping behavior as an excuse for doing poorly or failing than to put forth adequate effort and still do poorly or fail (as anticipated). The goal, ultimately, is to avoid as much of the chronic stress associated actual or anticipated negative academic outcomes as possible by externalizing (or excusing) those outcomes (i.e., blaming the self-handicapping behavior for our failure rather than our own inadequacy or lack of intelligence).

Experiencing complex trauma as a child or adolescent increases a student's vulnerability to overusing self-handicapping academic behavior because trauma-based neuroplasticity

76

compromises their natural ability to regulate negative emotions. Self-handicapping becomes an effective way to compensate for this compromised ability, at least academically (even though there are nonacademic self-handicapping behaviors). The negative emotions (and chronic stress) associated with anticipated, undesirable academic outcomes are now "regulated" (and even perceived as being controlled) by the self-handicapping behavior.

Complex trauma changes the "way that the prefrontal cortex, amygdala and hippocampus interact," noted David Hosier. These changes typically lead to "repetitive dysfunctional behavior that persists because it is so hard to unlearn." The chronic stress of complex trauma triggers continuous cortisol production which maladaptively increases the size and activity of the amygdala, while concurrently decreasing the size and activity of the hippocampus and prefrontal cortex. Students experiencing complex trauma will then be susceptible to heightened emotional reactivity due to a larger, hyperactive amygdala, especially since those brain structures (i.e., hippocampus and prefrontal cortex) that otherwise regulate negative emotion, memory, information processing, and impulsivity have been significantly diminished. Consequently, negative emotional reactions (e.g., anxiety, anger, frustration, hopelessness, helplessness) are easier to generate and harder to regulate properly.

The emotional reaction we recognize as anxiety is ridiculously important to the amygdala. Often mistaken for fear, anxiety is more so associated with the anticipation of a future-oriented threat (unlike fear which is a reaction to possibly being harmed in the present). Our amygdala is designed to remember the fear we have neuronally associated (i.e., neural circuitry is created or strengthened) with a certain life circumstance and revisit that fear whenever we re-experience the circumstance; thus, we establish a conditioned anxiety to certain tangible or psychological situations where it becomes harder to not fear them in advance.

Our fear response (also known as the stress response and the fight or flight response) to the threatening stimuli eventually becomes fixed in our brain as normal and necessary. Why? Our survival, of course. Once we fear a situation often or intensely enough, our amygdala begins to condition our brain to believe that the situation is inherently dangerous and record the fear we felt about it. Complex trauma (and trauma-based neuroplasticity) is actually rooted psychologically in chronic anxiety.

In other words, whenever we experience a recurring and/or traumatizing situation and typically react with the fear response, our amygdala forms an association between the situation and fear. The next time we're confronted with the situation, we will reflexively recall the fear we repeatedly or remarkably felt before and feel it again. We will automatically feel anxiety, and once we accept the anxiety (or simply refuse to not accept it), the neural association between the situation and this reaction is reinforced. And because this happens so quickly, we have very little conscious control over it. Oftentimes, even the anxiety—which inevitably becomes chronic—is unconscious.

A chronically anxious brain houses an overactivated (and hence *changed*) amygdala. This amygdala is on constant (albeit subconscious) alert for possible danger and is vulnerable to perceiving and overreacting to danger that may not actually be all that dangerous. The hypervigilant amygdala is constantly activating the stress response. Every activation makes a future activation much more likely (as it becomes patterned neuronal activity). Ultimately, the traumatic stress response is stuck *on* and the brain continues to change.

In a classroom full of *probably traumatized* Black or poor students, this implicit yet pervasive feeling of being under constant psychological (and sometimes even physical) threat and extreme vulnerability along with our students' impaired ability to regulate this feeling will not automatically seem trauma-based (even though it very much is). What trauma-based neuroplasticity does— especially when concentrated in high-poverty, high-minority schools—is manifest itself as an emotional atmosphere that reeks of a terribly consistent combination of overwhelmedness, fatigue,

78

frustration, disappointment, joylessness, hopelessness, anxiety, anger, neglect, shame, disrespect, hostility, and helplessness that has evolved into stubborn indifference.

These emotional responses, for the most part, are mutually experienced between trauma-ignorant educators (i.e., teachers and administrators) and their equally trauma-ignorant students (and, indirectly, these students' parents), all of whom struggle to believe they have a strong likelihood of achieving success in their respective roles. While educators can just flee or avoid high-poverty, high-minority schools, these trauma-based emotional responses tangibly manifest themselves among the students as "boredom with curricula, truancy, disciplinary problems, too much unstructured time, confused or unrealistic aspirations, insufficient perseverance, and low self-efficacy," observed Sally Reis et al.

It's critical to recall that "trauma is not an event in itself," explained Lenore Terr, "but is instead the reaction to extremely stressful life circumstances. When children operate in overwhelming states of stress, the stress response system may become the normal mode of functioning." Traumatic stress is an overwhelming state of stress resulting from a traumatic experience.

Stress (i.e., the stress response) is essentially an interaction between an external, negative stimulus and our brain's response, a response largely determined by the magnitude of the stimulus as compared to our personal (or social) competence or resources for dealing with the stimulus. Whenever we perceive (consciously or unconsciously, accurately or inaccurately) a negative discrepancy between the magnitude of the stimulus and our personal (or social) competence or resources to cope, we experience stress; if we perceive this discrepancy recurrently, then we experience *chronic* stress.

Elissa Epel et al. explained that "situations where a goal that matters to the person is at stake and the demands of the situation outweigh the person's resources for coping with it can cause feelings of 'stress.' We may feel 'stressed' when a situation harms or threatens important goals ('threat appraisals'). In contrast, in a stressful situation, a person might see the possibility of doing well at coping and thus perceive the stressor as a challenge ('challenge appraisals')." In other words, we run from threats (or deny them into presumptive oblivion). We confront challenges (only because we're emboldened by optimistic odds). It's the way we're wired (why risk survival?).

In the modern world, our stress is oftentimes directed at threats that will not necessarily (or at least not immediately) kill us, yet the fight or flight response is so hardwired into our neural circuitry that we typically react to those threats as if they were actually lethal. Most of us respond this exact way so habitually we're not even conscious of it. And this inclination can ultimately be destructive (i.e., produce negative neuroplasticity). According to Pamela J. Sawyer et al., "stress can be adaptive as it helps the body to meet the demands of the threatening situation. However, exposure to chronic stress can lead to allostatic load, the wear and tear on the [brain] produced through chronic or repeated activation of the stress-response systems."

Most people underestimate the validity or gravity of stress. "Stress is real," explained Jensen. It's the brain's cognitive, emotional, and behavioral reaction to actual or anticipated threats to our personal (i.e., physical, psychological, material) or social integrity and the fear of not having the resources to effectively respond to them.

Stress is not all bad, though. Some stress is actually constructive. In addition to preparing to fight or flee, stress also enables us to evolve in order to better adapt to our environment and experiences. Emotional reactivity mobilizes the attentive energy required for any significant adaptive response to an adverse environment or adverse experiences. If we don't change enough that our response to adversity becomes effective, we ultimately risk our own survival (which a survival-oriented brain simply can't allow, even if it requires unconscious, maladaptive responses that are "effective" simply because they enable survival). Our brain, as the essential organ of stress, also adapts (or changes) to traumatic or chronic stress (as it becomes patterned neuronal activity). In other words, stress both facilitates and is a byproduct of neuroplasticity.

A stressor is basically something (e.g., events, experiences, perceptions, or environmental demands) that instigates the stress response once we are exposed to it. In terms of cause and effect, stressors are the cause while stress is the effect. Once the brain recognizes the existence of a stressor, it reflexively initiates the most efficient survival strategy associated with that specific stressor.

In even nerdier neuroscientific terms, a stressor is any circumstance that threatens human homeostasis. For arguably the nerdiest description of a stressor, we turn to the originator of the term Hans Selye, who proposed that physical and "psychosocial stressors are defined principally by cognitive or affective components and reflect an anticipation of a looming challenge to homeostasis."

Key new term here: *homeostasis*. Homeostasis is a regulatory process by which humans (and living things in general) sustain the relative internal stability (i.e., optimal functioning of all internal systems) necessary for survival while concurrently responding to adverse and/or altering external stimuli. Stressors, by definition, are adverse and/or altering external stimuli that disrupt homeostasis. Stressors are anything that interrupts the relatively balanced functioning of the brain and/or body. The survival-oriented human brain is designed to maintain a state of homeostasis. Stress disturbs homeostasis as the stressor is dealt with. Chronic stress, as we'll see later, makes homeostasis virtually impossible (and *allostasis* potentially devastating).

Allostasis (or next key new term) is the reactionary process by which the human brain automatically compensates for stressful environmental stimuli in order to reestablish relative internal stability (i.e., homeostasis). While stress disrupts homeostasis, allostasis attempts to restore it. However, this attempt at restoring stability requires change (i.e., neuroplasticity).

81

Bruce McEwen and Peter Gianaros acknowledged that "the brain determines what is threatening, and hence stressful, to the individual; regulates the physiological, behavioral, cognitive, and emotional responses that an individual will deploy in order to cope with a given stressor via dynamic and plastic neural circuitry; and changes in its plasticity both adaptively and maladaptively as a result of coping with stressful experiences."

Allostasis is the process of attaining the relative internal stability (i.e., homeostasis) required for survival through physiological, behavioral, cognitive, emotional, and/or brain changes. According to David Borsook et al., "the brain responds to potential and actual stressful events by activating hormonal and neural mediators and modifying behaviors to adapt. Such responses help maintain physiological stability (allostasis). When behavioral or physiological stressors are frequent and/or severe, allostatic responses can become dysregulated and maladaptive (allostatic load). Allostatic load may alter brain networks both functionally and structurally. As a result, the brain's responses to continued/subsequent stressors are abnormal, and behavior and systemic physiology are altered in ways that can, in a vicious cycle, lead to further allostatic load."

Oftentimes a psychosocial stressor, in order to be sufficiently alleviated (and allostasis achieved), requires a coping response that is beyond what we are currently capable of generating. This is particularly true when the stressor is ambiguously negative, unpredictable, chronic, and uncontrollable; the stress it produces is actually aggravated.

Whenever we're not capable of coping effectively with certain stressors (especially traumatic stressors) and cannot accomplish allostasis, the consequence is a cumulative effect known as *allostatic load*. With allostatic load, instead of achieving relative internal stability, especially with regard to emotional regulation, overutilization of the stress response (and oversaturation of neural structures and circuitry by stress hormones) is *normalized* as patterned neuronal activity.

82

Our survival-oriented brain somehow becomes convinced that constantly being stressed is necessary for survival. Eventually, constantly being stressed (i.e., overactivating the stress response) can lead to an enduring inability to achieve homeostasis because the brain becomes stuck in perpetual allostasis. Allostatic load (or overload) is the neuroplastic result of our brain's chronic exposure to an exaggerated neural response due to continuous stress and allostasis. Neural pathways and structures (e.g., prefrontal cortex, hippocampus, and amygdala) are maladaptively changed as the brain is burdened by being constantly forced to adapt to abnormally recurrent adverse physical or psychosocial situations.

Javier Gilabert-Juan et al. asserted that chronic "aversive experiences, such as stress or fear" or trauma "can induce neuronal structural and functional plasticity" as a "neuroprotective mechanism." In other words, chronic stress or anxiety or trauma compels the brain to change in an attempt to preserve relatively normal neuronal structure and/or functioning (i.e., achieve homeostasis via allostasis). However, if these experiences and subsequent changes are too prolonged it makes returning to *normal* much more difficult. A new normal is established that may not provide adequate or appropriate adjustment to past experiences and may promote increased vulnerability to comparable experiences in the future.

For instance, when functioning properly (i.e., without the burden of chronic stress or anxiety), the amygdala directs incoming emotional information to the prefrontal cortex where it is logically evaluated for response or repression. The primary functions of the highly plastic prefrontal cortex (PFC) are the regulation of emotional behavior and the processing of external information in order to decide reasonable cognitive, behavioral, and emotional responses to the information. However, the altered neural circuitry of a chronically stressed or anxious amygdala experiencing allostasis load blocks the flow of information to the PFC. Instead, the amygdala's function is modified to now include the processing

83

of external information in order to decide cognitive, behavioral, and emotional responses to the information (in lieu of the PFC).

This is particularly maladaptive considering how inherently irrational any decisions led by the emotion-based amygdala must be. This functional change inevitably limits most cognitive, behavioral, and emotional responses to incoming emotional information—especially negative emotional information—to the repeated activation of the stress (i.e., fight or flight) response, which only aggravates the cumulative impact of additional stress on allostasis load. A pattern (i.e., patterned neuronal activity) is quickly established that leads to more persistent neuroplasticity and accompanying manifested behavioral changes.

Emotions (e.g., those associated with traumatic experiences) are equally as influential as experiences in the altering of neural circuitry. The brain experiences emotion (and traumatic stress) via the release of certain neurotransmitters (or brain chemicals) like adrenalin and dopamine as well as hormones such as cortisol. When neural structures and pathways are chronically awash with these brain chemicals and hormones, neural structures and pathways can be significantly changed structurally or functionally. Cortisol, the primary stress hormone, is secreted from the adrenal cortex (or adrenal glands) and, when too much is released, has a particularly dysfunctional neuroplastic impact on the hippocampus (as well as the prefrontal cortex and amygdala).

The stress response is designed to be a temporary reaction by the survival-oriented human brain to situations perceived to be immediately life threatening (i.e., acute stressors or trauma). Functionally, it is a mechanism of provisional allostasis intended to promptly return us to homeostasis once the threat has been overcome. According to Kelly McGonigal, the stress response "is designed to help us survive emergencies, fix solvable problems, or navigate temporary social circumstances. It focuses our attention and floods us with energy, but in a way that is not sustainable as a default way of functioning."

When constantly activated due to chronic stress, the human stress response can evolve into a persistent state of neurophysiological hyperarousal. The neural circuitry and structures responsible for producing the stress response are altered to become the dominant areas of the chronically stressed individual's brain. Chronic stress is a significant catalyst for neuroplasticity. Chronic stress, according to Machiko Matsumoto and Hiroko Togashi, changes the human brain by creating "long-lasting alterations in the neural circuits underlying emotional regulation and increase the subsequent reactivity to stress later in life."

Chronic stress can result from mundane everyday stressors as well as exceptionally traumatic events. The key to chronic stress is the presence of control over the stressor; chronic stress also tends to be uncontrollable stress. Logically, if we could control the stressor, we would almost certainly stop it before it becomes chronic stress.

Stress, by definition, is the brain's response to the perception of uncontrollability resulting from a threatening situation. The mere perception of control over a stressor mitigates the neuroplastic impact of the stress response. Conversely, the presumption of uncontrollability over a recurrent stressor can induce a condition called *learned helplessness*, which can aggravate the neuroplastic impact of the stress response. The human brain is not constructed to efficiently deal with prolonged stress that seems uncontrollable.

It is the repetitiveness of chronic stress that changes the human brain (by becoming patterned neuronal activity), arguably more than anything else (excluding everything that happens in the first few years of life). Chronic stress creates lasting, pathological changes in both brain structure and functioning, especially in the highly interconnected neural circuitry of the amygdala, prefrontal cortex, and hippocampus.

Chronic stress causes the brain to change its physical response to stress. Acute stress causes the release of cortisol, a hormone designed to enable the brain to elevate blood sugar and pressure levels in order to enhance our ability to respond to danger. Without cortisol, the survival-oriented brain couldn't be survival-oriented. However, with chronic stress there is so much cortisol constantly being produced, it basically becomes meaningless to the normal neural circuitry. The brain has to recalculate what it considers an abnormal amount of cortisol just to sustain its ability to respond reflexively to serious threat.

Constant cortisol saturation significantly changes neural structures like the hippocampus and PFC, both of which are gradually reduced in size and activity as cortisol annihilates hippocampus and PFC neurons via prolonged overactivation. Conversely, continuous cortisol production increases the size and activity of the amygdala. According to research by Christopher Pittenger and Ronald Duman, "chronic stress enhances synaptic plasticity and the function of amygdala neurons, an effect quite distinct from the atrophy it induces in the hippocampus and PFC. This could both result from and contribute to overactivation of neuronal circuits that control fear, anxiety, and emotion."

The now hyperactive and hypertrophied amygdala promotes persistent states of hypervigilance and heightened emotional reactivity, even our stress response is exacerbated. Chronic stress strengthens the neural pathway between the amygdala and hippocampus and weakens the neural pathway between the hippocampus and prefrontal cortex. Consequently, our fight or flight response to perceived threats is drastically quickened because our ability to moderate it is linked to the functional efficiency of the hippocampus and prefrontal cortex, both of which are neuronally atrophied by continuous cortisol saturation. In other words, an exaggerated stress response is a consequence of the brain changes brought about by chronic stress (i.e., people who stress a lot tend to continue to stress a lot).

The enhanced connection between the amygdala and hippocampus makes us considerably more anxious (i.e., threats appear ubiquitous and overstated); thus, chronic anxiety is an additional consequence of the brain changes brought about by chronic stress. Constant cortisol saturation reinforces the neural circuitry connecting the amygdala and hippocampus, which effectively creates a brain predisposed to existing in a perpetual state of fight or flight (as well as allostasis).

As aforementioned, constant activation of the autonomic nervous system and hypothalamic-pituitary-adrenal (or HPA) axis (i.e., constant allostasis) is an effect of chronic stress. Constant allostasis inevitably produces allostatic load. Allostatic load causes neuronal atrophy in the hippocampus and PFC and neuronal hypertrophy in the amygdala. These are significant structural (i.e., neuronal size) and functional (i.e., neuronal excitability) changes in the brain. Rick Nauert recognized that the hippocampus and PFC are "necessary for processing information about the controllability of stressors as well as applying this information to regulate responses to subsequent stressors." Having an undersized hippocampus and PFC can make people more susceptible to stress and anxiety throughout their lives, essentially creating an inertia-like effect on their stress response (i.e., people who stress/fear a lot tend to continue to stress/fear a lot, even if they're not conscious of it).

Chronic stress-induced plasticity in the aforementioned neural structures and pathways can lead to long-term difficulty regulating negative emotions (i.e., diminished control of negative emotion). Research led by Supriya Ghosh shows that chronic stress rewires our brain to "discount factual information and to rely heavily on emotional experiences" and memories. This is a result of the hyperactivation and hypertrophy of the amygdala and concurrent hypoactivation and atrophy of the hippocampus and prefrontal cortex.

As fear and other negative emotions begin to trump cognition, how we feel (and how we don't want to feel) becomes more important than what we know and how we know it. "Emotional information is prioritized and receives privileged access to attention and awareness," explained Patrik Vuilleumier. Problem solving becomes far less of a priority than fighting or fleeing (or denying). Not an ideal brain orientation, especially for members of socioeconomically disadvantaged groups prone to experiencing a lifetime of disproportionately negative emotions and experiences.

"Emotional processes not only serve to record the value of sensory events, but also to elicit adaptive responses and modify perception. Recent research using functional brain imaging in human subjects has begun to reveal neural substrates by which sensory processing and attention can be modulated by the affective significance of stimuli. The amygdala plays a crucial role in providing both direct and indirect top-down signals on sensory pathways, which can influence the representation of emotional events, especially when related to threat."

Our brain's natural capacity for regulating its reaction to negative emotions is essential, not just for survival but for success in anything. Chronic stress-induced neuroplasticity terribly compromises this ability. Rather than our emotions running our lives (while changing our brains), Camara Harrell et al. explained that "emotional regulation refers to the ability to increase, maintain, or inhibit the expression and experience of an emotional response." When we can efficiently regulate our negative emotions, we influence if, when, and how we experience and (our brains) are affected by them. When we can't, negative emotions can negatively bias our thoughts and actions; they can control us rather than the other way around.

Our capacity for emotional self-regulation depends heavily on the functional efficiency of the neural circuitry connecting the prefrontal cortex and amygdala. This connectivity is compromised dramatically in the brains of people who have experienced chronic stress.

Emotional self-regulation is the ability to react to negative emotional stimuli (including traumatic stress) without compromising our long-term best interest, which typically means inhibiting our reflexive response in favor of a more appropriate one. When this ability is intact, we can scrutinize and manage our

88

own emotions, thoughts, and actions as well as constructively modify them when circumstances require it. Emotional regulation also includes the capacity to persist in significant tasks even when we don't get pleasure from doing so.

"Though it is possible for children to recover from traumatic experiences and regain control of their behavioral responses through intervention and support," concluded Travis Wright, "research on the traumatic response suggests that traumatized children's behavior is not always under their control. When children operate in overwhelming states of stress," such as complex traumatic stress, "the stress response system may become the normal mode of functioning."

Consequently, "even when actual dangers are not present, children may react to the world as if they are. Unable to control their heightened levels of emotional response and arousal, traumatized children simply cannot turn off the survival strategies being employed by their brains. Over time, the notion that one must be on constant guard becomes internalized, with many traumatized children coming to school every day in survival mode. They anticipate that the classroom environment will be threatening and spend their days scanning for any warning of danger" (i.e., psychological threats), just like many of their possibly also and/or vicariously[20] traumatized teachers who semiconsciously equate difficult/Black/poor students with danger.

---

[20]   Vicarious (or secondary) trauma, explained Ray Wolpow et al., results from "internalizing the traumatizing event experienced by another" (e.g., traumatized students). "It is not uncommon for school professionals, who have a classroom with one or more students struggling with the effects of trauma, to experience symptoms very much like those their students are exhibiting. These symptoms are called vicarious or secondary trauma. (Vicarious: to feel through the experience of others; a secondary experience of the trauma rather than primary one.) It can affect...our ability to reason, our ability to be empathetic, and how we relate to others" (especially our traumatized students). Awareness and self-care (e.g., regular peer support,

Complex trauma typically experienced by our students outside of the classroom creates attitudes and behavioral reactions that interfere with learning inside the classroom. Because of neuroplasticity, the "most developed areas of a child's brain are the ones used most frequently," concluded Susan Cole et al. For students experiencing complex trauma, the neural pathways and structures associated with the traumatic stress response oftentimes become overdeveloped through constant triggering. "These parts of the brain may direct behavior even in situations in which it would be more appropriate for other parts of the brain to be in charge." The regions of the brain active in trauma are "different from those active in calm states, and it is predominately the areas active in calm states that are required for academic learning."

Some students experience childhood trauma, even complex trauma, and their experience doesn't automatically trigger trauma-based maladaptive neuroplasticity and the aforementioned impulsiveness, emotional dysregulation, and negative classroom behaviors. There's not a uniform response to experiencing childhood trauma; some youth are more resilient than others with regard to their access to internal and external resources to cope with and recover from the experience.

Unfortunately, more often than not, Black or poor students experience some type of complex trauma (at least, but usually in addition to, race-based experiences or intergenerational poverty) that inevitably prompts significant maladaptive neuroplasticity. This is largely because their trauma resilience has been compromised by not having adequate access to those aforementioned internal and external resources or a locus of control or hope not diminished by the flagrant uncontrollability of racism or intergenerational poverty.

Neuroplasticity—also known as brain plasticity, neuronal plasticity, cerebral plasticity, cortical remapping, or cortical

---

meditation, exercise, healthy eating, prioritizing sleep, professional counseling, engaging in activities and hobbies we enjoy) can minimize vicarious trauma.

plasticity—is the neural circuitry in the human brain's ability to change and adjust as a result of our environment, thoughts, emotions, lessons learned, observations, actions, (over)reactions, and experiences (e.g., trauma). Just to be clear, it does not mean that our brains are literally made of plastic. It does mean, to quote Paula Tallal, that "you create your brain from the input you get." Our brain is reconstructed to process any new or repetitive information, and if deemed useful (especially for survival), to retain it. For instance, your brain has markedly changed from the information you've read thus far in this book; certain neural circuitry in your brain have been created or changed (and who you are has been slightly altered).

Bryan Kolb and Ian Whishaw wrote that "brain plasticity refers to the brain's ability to change structure and function. Experience is a major stimulant of brain plasticity in animal species as diverse as humans. It is now clear that experience produces multiple, dissociable changes in the brain including increases in neuronal dendritic length, increases (or decreases) in spine density, synapse formation, increased glial activity, and altered metabolic activity. These anatomical neuronal changes are correlated with behavioral differences between subjects with and without the changes. Experience-dependent changes in neurons are affected by various factors" including traumatic stress.

Our brain, as explained by Kolstad, "deletes old connections between neurons and enables the creation of new ones. Through 'synaptic pruning,' connections that are inefficient or infrequently used fade away, while connections between neurons that are highly routed will be preserved and strengthened. In response to a new experience or novel information, neuroplasticity allows either an alteration to the structure of already-existing connections between neurons, or forms brand-new connections. The latter leads to increased synaptic density while the former makes existing pathways more efficient or suitable."

"The brain is remolded to collect and preserve the new data and, if useful, retain it. When we perceive the new information as especially important or when a certain experience is repeated fairly often the structural change in the brain will last and the new information is hardwired into the neural pathways of the brains. These changes result either in an alteration to an existing brain pathway, or in the formation of a new one. Further repetition of the same information or experience may lead to more modifications in the connections that house it, or an increase in the number of connections that can access it—again, as a result of the plasticity."

Doidge proclaimed neuroplasticity as "one of the most extraordinary discoveries of the twentieth century. Up until the discovery of neuroplasticity, scientists believed that the only way that the brain changes its structure is through evolution of the species, which in most cases takes many thousands of years. According to modern Darwinian evolutionary theory, new biological brain structures develop in a species when genetic mutations arise, creating variation in the gene pool. If these variations have survival value, they are more likely to be passed on to the next generation. But plasticity creates a new way—beyond mutation and variation—of introducing new biological brain structures in individuals by non-Darwinian means."

Polish neuroscientist Jerzy Konorski is credited with coining the term *neuroplasticity*, although the concept was developed concurrently yet independently by Konorski and Canadian neuropsychologist Donald Hebb in the late 1940s. Neuroplasticity, Sharon Begley explained, "means just what the two parts of the word would suggest, *neuro* refers to the brain and *plasticity* refers to the ability of the brain to change itself, to change its structure and function." Before Konorski and Hebb it was generally accepted that the adult human brain was a structurally and functionally static organ; it didn't change after early childhood. The work of these two men eventually convinced the neuroscientific community that the brain continually changes throughout our lifetime.

The human brain is not at all static. James Zull wrote that "the brain is molded and reshaped by the forces of life acting on it. Our wiring grows and develops depending on what we experience" directly or even vicariously. As a result of neuroplasticity, remarkable or recurring thoughts, emotions, observations, actions, (over)reactions, and experiences effectively become neurostructure. Whenever we have a new or chronic experience or thought, specific neurons are activated, neurotransmitters are released, new neural pathways are formed, and associated neural structures are functionally or structurally altered. Despite the survival-oriented intent of these changes, neuroplasticity can ultimately be either beneficial or maladaptive.

The human brain is literally formed (and reformed) under the influence of external and internal stimuli on neural pathways, functions, and structures. Consider your brain as a vast series of continually forming circuits (or wires). Each circuit is a chain of aroused neurons. Neurons are the primary cells of the brain (the other type of brain cell are glial cells, which exist only to maintain neurons), each enclosed by branches (or dendrites) that send and receive electrochemical signals (i.e., information) from other neurons. Each neural circuit distinctively affects our cognitive, emotional, or behavioral responses to the circumstances of our lives. These circuits are created by our experiences, especially those experiences associated with stress. In fact, most of our neural circuits are formed either throughout our first three years of life or when we experience chronic stress.

Experience changes our brain by activating or overacting certain neurons or neural structures as well as altering neural circuitry. When we consistently or intensely experience something, the neurons in our brain associated with our action or reaction to that experience *fire* (i.e., are activated) repeatedly. When neurons fire repeatedly, they grow (or more specifically, their dendrites grow) and extend themselves out toward other neurons, eventually forming neural connections (or circuitry) via the connecting neurons' synapses. The new neural circuitry sends electrochemical signals back and forth over billions of connected neurons within specific areas or structures in our brain. Neural circuitry processes information and mediates human behavior.

Begley explained that "the brain devotes more cortical real estate to functions that its owner uses more frequently and shrinks the space devoted to activities rarely performed. In response to the actions and experiences of its owner, a brain forges stronger connections in circuits that underlie one behavior or thought and weakens the connections in others. Most of this happens because of what we do and what we experience of the outside world. In this sense, the very structure of our brain—the relative size of different regions, the strength of connections between one area and another, even their functions—reflects the lives we have led."

Several brain regions and structures possess varying levels of structural and functional plasticity with regard to chronic traumatic stress triggered by experiencing complex trauma, including the amygdala, hippocampus, and prefrontal cortex.

An almond-shaped neural structure centrally located in the medial anterior temporal lobe, the amygdala (which is actually Greek for "almond") processes external stimuli and reflexively determines an emotional significance and response to that stimuli (particularly when deemed threatening), which is then sent out to other regions of the brain. The amygdala is directly associated with learned emotional responses (e.g., fear, anger, hopelessness, helplessness) and is *proportionately plastic*, which means chronic overactivation of neurons in the amygdala caused by complex trauma enlarges and hypersensitizes the amygdala (by strengthening its internal and outbound neural circuitry) which causes excessive, conditioned emotional reactions to recurrent (and potentially threatening or even traumatic) stimuli.

In other words, the more we repeatedly react emotionally to (or are overwhelmed emotionally by) life experiences, the more likely we are to react (or be overwhelmed) equally emotionally to those same or similar life experiences in the future because of changes to our amygdala. These reactions can become adaptive or maladaptive, more likely the latter as reacting emotionally subdues rational thought and authentic problem solving.

Terribly efficient, the amygdala can intuitively recognize associations between an incoming stimulus and salient stimuli-response patterns stored in our long-term memory and then facilitate a behavioral response to that stimulus based on patterned neuronal activation.

In many ways the amygdala is the centerpiece of our survival-oriented brain; it is the region principally responsible for the fight or flight (or stress) response. Not only does the amygdala facilitate our response to potentially threatening (or traumatic) stimuli, it also initiates the retention of effective (i.e., survival securing) stimuli-response patterns in our long-term memory. The amygdala automatically remembers what we did to survive (i.e., how we responded to threatening stimuli) and creates/strengthens neural circuitry to motivate us to repeat these emotions and behaviors without requiring rational thinking. The goal is to accelerate our response time to threatening stimuli and maximize our odds of survival by creating neural circuitry that enables instinctive reactions to ominous life circumstances.

Because of its designed efficiency, the amygdala reacts to external stimuli emotionally much quicker than the more rational regions of the brain can. Its speed comes from its ability to make decisions regarding our survival unconsciously. Humans can overrule our primarily amygdala-based response to life circumstances, but that requires acknowledging the amygdala's priority of response as well as practicing mindfulness with regard to making behavioral decisions based on reason rather than emotions. The survival orientation of the human brain makes this easier said than done; being logical is not as hardwired in the human brain as fighting or fleeing (or denying) is.

Adjacent to the amygdala, the hippocampus (a coupling of the Greek words "hippo" for horse and "kampos" for sea; so yes, it's shaped like a seahorse) somewhat functions as its ally. The hippocampus is where, among other things, long-term emotional memories as well as recollections of repeated emotional responses are created and stored. The hippocampus connects emotions (most of which originate from the amygdala) to memories. Emotional memories are the easiest to retain and recall. We remember emotional situations better because we also remember how they made us feel. The stronger (and more negative) the emotion associated with a situation, the stronger the resulting memory.

Experiences producing survival-oriented emotions (e.g., traumatic stress) are the most memorable because these memories are reinforced by the concurrent activation of the amygdala. It's only logical that a survival-oriented brain would be most proficient at recalling threatening experiences. This is valuable information. When information is deemed lastingly valuable (i.e., relevant to our future), the hippocampus connects the essential elements of that experience together and forms a permanent memory. Humans create permanent memories mostly to solve future problems; memories are cognitively efficient. Memories typically become a guide for future survival-oriented thoughts and behaviors.

A byproduct of patterned neuronal activity (i.e., newly created or reorganized neural circuitry), memories—particularly emotional memories—change (or represent changes in) the human brain, specifically the hippocampus. We remember because our neural circuitry changes; each memory primes the brain for a future experience because our neural circuitry has changed. Our thoughts, observations, emotions, actions, and (over)reactions are all influenced by what we remember of our past. Our emotional memories also impact what associations we are most vulnerable to making and internalizing in the future.

Cornelius Gross and Rene Hen observed that a decreased hippocampus size is "a direct consequence of the chronic state of stress. A smaller hippocampus increases an individual's susceptibility to environmental stress" by diminishing its natural ability to limit cortisol production. Chronic exposure to cortisol leads to neuronal shrinkage of the hippocampus, which functionally hampers the hippocampus's ability to create new emotional memories and limits us to reacting behaviorally based on preexisting memories. This makes us extremely vulnerable to *reflexively* reactivating stress responses (as opposed to our problem-solving faculty) whenever we experience novel life situations resembling past emotional situations (linked to anticipated negative outcomes) and aggravating allostatic load in our brain.

Connected to the hippocampus near the front of our brain is the prefrontal cortex (which isn't Greek for anything by the way). The prefrontal cortex (or PFC) functions as the relatively logical decision maker of the trio. It also regulates impulsive behavior and determines what decisions we make in response to emotional reactions (from the amygdala) and emotional memories (from the hippocampus). The PFC slows down our otherwise automatic responses (e.g., stress, anxiety) just long enough so we can regulate them and not be completely impulsive.

The overactivation of our amygdala and hippocampus concurrently underdevelops (i.e., reduces the neural functionality of) the PFC. As the amygdala and hippocampus are neuronally strengthened through repeated activation (e.g., being scared or stressed a lot), the prefrontal cortex is effectively weakened. Because it's highly plastic, an underdeveloped prefrontal cortex can lead to a reduced ability to regulate negative thinking and emotions as well as an increase in emotional and behavioral impulsivity.

When unimpacted by chronic traumatic stress, the prefrontal cortex, noted Pickens and Tschopp, regulates our "stress response by ensuring an individual is accurately reading a situation and making the best decision in response to a perceived threat." After experiencing complex trauma, a student's brain may sustain an exaggerated stress response, interfering with the PFC's ability to "operate and ultimately contributing to a perpetual mental state of being in 'survival mode.'"

Consequently, the student is now vulnerable to "constantly being triggered into a survival mode mindset," particularly when

97

confronted by highly negative, chronically stressful classroom emotions (e.g. overwhelmedness, fatigue, frustration, disappointment, joylessness, hopelessness, anxiety, anger, neglect, shame, disrespect, and helplessness). Any of these emotions may repetitively trigger "reminders of trauma that a student may or may not be aware exist," but still intuitively feels the need to survive psychologically. Their brains ultimately maladapt (i.e., change negatively) in order to merely survive these chronically stressful emotions, many of which are actually consequences of negative or unwitting teacher behaviors. And their brains, because of a past trauma, are inclined to exaggerate the priority of psychological survival regardless of the situation, even over academic success or possible punishment (e.g., better to survive and fail or be suspended than not survive).

The behaviors prompted by students' unconscious attempts to self-protect are most obvious when their capacity to emotionally self-regulate is overwhelmed by the perceived negativity of another person (e.g., other students, teacher, administrator), which initiates an overreaction to this perception. Students experiencing trauma-based neuroplasticity tend to react defensively to negative emotional stimuli in one of two ways: they will either retreat in fear, shame, or distractive behavior or they will aggress or act out in frustration, anger, and despair. Their classroom behavior, confirmed Jensen, usually "comes off as apathetic or rude but may actually indicate feelings of hopelessness or despair." These students tend to interpret certain academic "stressors as evidence of circumstances worsening or becoming more hopeless," which may trigger (or sustain) the traumatic stress response.

Any school experience that makes these students feel unintelligent, inadequate, incompetent, or exposed could trigger (or sustain) the traumatic stress response, including implicitly negative teacher expectations. Teacher expectations are typically biased by past student behavior or academic performance (which for probably traumatized students would already be compromised by trauma-based neuroplasticity) coupled with whatever stereotypes or stigma are associated with their students (e.g., race, poverty).

"If I'm a teacher and decide that a student isn't any good, I may be communicating that to the student," noted Seth Gershenson. "A teacher communicating to a student they're not smart will weigh heavily on how that student feels about their future and perhaps the effort they put into doing well in school." Oftentimes, a student experiencing complex trauma "may modify their self-expectations, and in turn their behavior, to conform to teachers' negative biases," especially when they "lack access to role models who could counteract a teacher's low expectations."

Most teachers are neither crass nor conscious (of their biased expectations or trauma itself) enough to blatantly or verbally communicate negative expectations exclusively to their probably traumatized Black or poor students. To cite Kathleen Cotton, "as with the formation of expectations based on inappropriate factors, the communication of differential expectations is often unconscious on the part of teachers." However, as a teacher it is extremely difficult, if not impossible, to consistently conceal your expectations. Even when *you're* not conscious of your expectations, your students may very well be (especially those students already hypervigilant from experiencing trauma).

Teacher expectations of their students often create what Robert Tauber refers to as "expectation-revealing perceiver expressive behaviors"—behaviors that suggest to someone what we expect from them. These expressive behaviors may be verbal or nonverbal, unintentional or deliberate. Either way, our "expectations influence such expressive behaviors, and these behaviors influence the actions of others." Negative teacher expectations are a specific type of negative (or threatening) external stimuli. Students experiencing trauma-based neuroplasticity consequently have brains that are especially perceptive to and preoccupied with negative external stimuli.

"Human beings of all ages, including children, are uncanny at being able to tell what others think they are capable of doing and/or achieving.   Students acquire information about their abilities by observing their teachers' differential treatment of high and low achievers.   No matter what the source of information, whether it be verbal and/or nonverbal, the fact is that most of us are capable of deciphering what it is that others expect from us." When students acknowledge these verbal and nonverbal expectations, and if they are consistently and highly negative, the expectations themselves can become an additional source of chronic traumatic stress.

Our implicit expectations, which oftentimes conflict with our declared expectations, for our students are very hard to hide from them, largely because the former tend to be mostly negative.

Kevin McGrew and Jeffrey Evans observed that "although most teachers report that they can fully control their behavioral affect and deceive students whenever necessary, at times the two primary modes of communication [verbal and nonverbal] can send mixed signals.   Communication 'leakage' is present when an individual tries to conceal a particular affect (e.g., negative) toward another individual by consciously controlling their obvious communication behavior (e.g., speech content).   But the opposite message (i.e., negative affect) can still be transmitted via less controllable communication behavior (e.g., the face and then the body).   Furthermore, research has suggested that when people try to consciously conceal negative affect and instead transmit false-positive affect, the deceit is more successful in the controllable channels (e.g., speech content) and not as successful in less controllable channels (e.g., the face and then the body)."

Once coupled with other adverse childhood experiences and academic circumstances[21] all too common to Black and poor

---

[21]   To include lower teacher quality; a less impactful curriculum; lower per pupil expenditures; less effective classroom management; an overreliance on exclusionary discipline; higher student-to-teacher ratios; less access to new books, computers, the Internet, and other resources that stimulate or improve student engagement; a school climate generally less conducive to learning; practically nonexistent (or negligible at best)

students, negative teacher expectations as an additional chronic traumatic stressor can remarkably limit their likelihood of academic success by further prompting maladaptive neuroplasticity that reduces these students' capacity to regulate negative emotions and impulsivity. Chronic traumatic stressors, explained Ernest Izard, "cause the lower brain to focus on survival while slowing down the prefrontal cortex," which ultimately becomes underdeveloped and incapable of consistently supporting proper emotional regulation.

Chronic traumatic stress "changes the brain dramatically," concluded Jensen. It specifically changes how our brain attempts to internally process negative emotions as external stimuli. Chronic traumatic stress can trigger continuous cortisol production which maladaptively increases the size and activity of the amygdala (while decreasing the size and activity of the hippocampus and prefrontal cortex). Consequently, negative emotional reactions (e.g., anxiety, anger, frustration, hopelessness, helplessness) are easier to generate and harder to regulate. A compromised capacity to emotionally self-regulate can increase students experiencing complex trauma *artificial* inclination "to avoid challenge and to give up or withdraw effort," noted Bahram Jowkar et al., "especially when they are low in perceived competence."

These students stop taking enough of the positive academic risks (e.g., giving maximum effort, effectually responding to teacher checks for understanding, adequately studying for assessments, taking advantage of academic supports as needed) required for learning. Their brain tends to uniquely process these risks as most likely becoming shame-inducing experiences based on the perceived psychological threat of anticipated inadequacy and failure. Such experiences, like their previous or ongoing trauma, are expected to somehow overwhelm their "capacity to regulate their emotions" and "ability to cope with what they have

parental engagement and trust in the academic process; and significant (yet otherwise preventable) knowledge gaps.

101

experienced" and, consequently, become traumatic (or trauma triggers).

Trauma-informed educators are better equipped to not simply over-penalize probably traumatized students for disproportionately displaying negative emotions and emotionally dysregulated classroom behavior due to traumatic stress reactions, while still holding them accountable for high academic and behavioral expectations via strategic interventions and supports. "Punishment alone...doesn't change behavior," noted John Snelgrove, especially behavior stemming from trauma-based maladaptive neuroplasticity.

Human thought and behavior are explicitly impacted by our emotions. James Gross described emotions as "brief responses affecting both behavior as well as the brain that are generated during events with the potential to present challenges or opportunities."

The primary purpose of emotions is to promote survival by motivating us to (re)act quickly with minimal thinking in ways that will maximize our chances for survival. Shawn Radcliffe explained that "every area that has been found to be connected to emotions also has a role in cognition. So, our emotions and our ability to think are intertwined."

Emotions are associated with areas or structures in our brain that focus our attention on the threat, prompt (or motivate) specific survival-oriented actions, and determine the threatening implications of the external circumstances of our lives. The brain experiences emotion via the release of certain neurotransmitters (or brain chemicals) like adrenalin and dopamine as well as hormones such as cortisol. When neural structures and pathways are chronically awash with these brain chemicals and hormones due to repeatedly negative experiences (i.e., complex trauma), neural structures and pathways can be significantly changed structurally or functionally.

Peter Lang et al. explained that "emotions are considered to be action dispositions. It is held that affects evolved from reflexive, overt reactions to appetitive or aversive stimulation that served immediate survival functions (e.g., nurturance, sexual approach, fight, flight). The neural mechanisms for these functions are preserved in the human brain in subcortical and deep cortical structures, and are the foundation of human emotion. Expressed emotions developed from primitive actions that facilitated the survival of species and individuals. In man, the evolved affects are best characterized as motivationally tuned states of readiness. Although emotions may come in many forms…their fundamental organization is motivational."

Emotions are largely internal responses to external circumstances; negative circumstances instigate negative emotions. Because there generally are more things in our lives trying to end or oppress said lives than not (i.e., negative circumstances), we experience more negative emotions than positive ones.

Negative emotions can also instigate quite a bit of maladaptive neuroplasticity. The human brain reacts more dynamically to external stimuli it deems negative. "Negative stimuli produce more neural activity than positive stimuli," explained Jeff Haden. Negative information is processed more rapidly and thoroughly than positive or neutral information. "Across an array of psychological situations and tasks," according to Amrisha Vaish et al., "humans display a negativity bias, or the propensity to attend to, learn from, and use negative information far more than positive information." This bias is inherent to the human brain's neural circuitry. Our brain evolved to react more instantaneously and intensely to threat and anxiety than to ambition and opportunity.

"At a higher cognitive level, negative stimuli are hypothesized to carry greater informational value than positive stimuli, and to thus require greater attention and cognitive processing. Accordingly, humans spend more time looking at negative than at positive stimuli, perceive negative stimuli to be more complex than positive ones, and form more complex cognitive representations of negative than of positive stimuli."

103

Our negativity bias is actually an ancient survival mechanism. Much of humanity's survival-oriented behaviors involve simply avoiding danger. This particular cognitive bias causes our brain to be on constant, default alert for potential threats so that we are especially motivated to continue to avoid danger.

Rick Hanson wrote that while our inborn negativity bias "primes us for avoidance," it also cultivates and exaggerates other negative emotions, such as shame, frustration, anger, anxiety, and hopelessness. "It highlights past losses and failures, downplays present abilities, and exaggerates future obstacles."

The amygdala is essentially the brain's most negative neural structure (as well as apparently the most plastic). The amygdala triggers our negative emotional responses to negatively perceived circumstances faster than (and without) our conscious awareness. It is, to quote Tom Moon, "neurologically primed to label experiences as frightening and threatening." Two out of every three neurons in the amygdala are geared toward perceiving experiences negatively, and then immediately stockpiling these experiences as long-term memories, which are eventually used to instinctively assess potential threats (as probable threats or trauma).

Ultimately, it creates the neurostructure that yields increased vulnerability to negative emotions (and trauma), as past negative emotions negatively bias our emotional reaction to future experiences. The more potential negativity we experience, the larger and more active the neurons of the amygdala becomes. Chronic negativity (i.e., the incessant triggering of negative emotions) changes the amygdala by generating continuous cortisol overproduction. Continuous cortisol overproduction increases the neuronal size and activity of the amygdala (i.e., targeted neuroplasticity).

The consequently hyperactive and hypertrophied amygdala promotes persistent states of heightened negative emotional reactivity, causing even more cortisol to be released along with more neuroplasticity. The functionally and structurally augmented amygdala is constantly triggering negative emotions in response to circumstances it is now more inclined to perceive negatively, and every negative emotional response makes future negative emotional responses much more likely (as it becomes patterned neuronal activity).

Amygdalar plasticity can lead to long-term difficulty regulating negative emotions (i.e., diminished control of negative emotions). Chronic overactivation of neurons in the amygdala enlarges and hypersensitizes the amygdala (by strengthening its internal and outbound neural circuitry) which causes excessive, conditioned emotional reactions to external stimuli.

In other words, the more we repeatedly react negatively and emotionally to life circumstances, the more likely we are to react negatively and emotionally to those same (or similar) life circumstances in the future because of changes to our brain, specifically our amygdala. These repeated reactions become patterned neuronal activity in which certain negative emotions are paired with specific external stimuli (or life circumstances) in order to increases the probability of a negatively emotional response. Reacting with negative emotions becomes our default and habitual response to most external stimuli (or life circumstances).

Chronic traumatic stress strengthens the neural pathway between the amygdala and hippocampus and weakens the neural pathway between the hippocampus and prefrontal cortex. Consequently, our fight or flight response to perceived traumatic threats (or traumatic reminders) is drastically quickened because our ability to moderate this response is linked to the functional efficiency of the hippocampus and prefrontal cortex, both of which are neuronally atrophied by continuous cortisol saturation. In other words, an exaggerated traumatic stress response is a consequence of the brain changes brought about by experiencing chronic traumatic stress.

However, trauma-informed educators can strategically provide academic experiences that improve probably trauma-affected

105

students' test scores while simultaneously building their capacity for emotional self-regulation. In fact, these educators recognize that not gradually building this capacity compromises the likelihood that student test scores will ever improve.

The "ability to self-regulate or modulate emotions is a key predictor of academic success," confirmed Susan Cole et al., largely because this ability ultimately increases academic resilience and prevents overreliance on self-handicapping academic behaviors. Yet, a "lack of capacity for emotional self-regulation," noted Sheree Toth and Dante Cicchetti, "is probably the most striking feature" of students experiencing complex trauma. "Unlike the nontraumatized child, the hypervigilant child cannot shift away from distressing cues in the service of maintaining emotional regulation." As aforementioned, this hypervigilance is a consequence of trauma-based maladaptive neuroplasticity.

Students experiencing complex trauma and emotional dysregulation tend to protect their trauma-distorted self-concept from potentially overwhelming negative classroom emotions by overusing self-handicapping academic behaviors. Specifically, these students use self-handicapping behaviors to cope with the potentially traumatic psychological threat of anticipated inadequacy and failure. This anticipation stems from a self-concept already compromised by past or ongoing trauma.[22]

---

[22]   Our psychological reaction to complex childhood trauma oftentimes includes exceptionally devaluing our self-concept. Done unconsciously, this devaluation is intended to *defend* our self-concept from the traumatic stress of self-blame by "attributing exaggerated negative qualities to self," explained Randall Wickham and Janet West. In other words, whatever childhood trauma we've experienced is our fault because we somehow don't possess enough of whatever positive qualities would have prevented the trauma. A devalued self-concept is a distinct consequence of C-PTSD (or complex trauma-based neuroplasticity) whenever the devaluation is associated with complex trauma. The traumatized child concludes that there is something deeply wrong with

106

For Black or poor students, this threat is exaggerated by racial stigma or the stigma of intergenerational poverty. When students experience the stigma associated with Blackness in America or intergenerational poverty, they concurrently experience the omnipresent, ominous expectation of anticipated inadequacy and failure. Because of stigma, the expectations for Black or poor people are generally negative as well as inadequacy and failure-oriented. Racial inequality and intergenerational poverty are perceived as somehow their fault, a consequence of their own inherent inadequacy and individual failure rather than systemic racism, White privilege, deindustrialization-based joblessness, and the incessant wealth gap in contemporary America.

Hastily labeled by educators as (innately) incompetent, indifferent, or even incorrigible, many *probably traumatized* Black and poor students are actually "self-worth protective students who struggle with a debilitating fear of failure." In effect, to quote Ted Thompson and Zoe Perry, "their fear of failure is so strong that they will use self-handicapping behaviors such as withholding effort to avoid the risk of failure."

Being "self-protective" is these students' defensive reaction to the perceived inevitably or expectation of inadequacy and failure. They "withhold effort to protect themselves from experiencing failure" and inadequacy. In other words, they avoid academic experiences that potentially generate feelings of failure and inadequacy. However, the academic underdevelopment (i.e., knowledge gaps) that results from avoidance tends to reinforce the initial fear of failure and inadequacy.

Uncertain self-worth is "known to be critical in relation to self-handicapping behaviors. People who are uncertain of their overall self-worth are likely to sabotage their performance intentionally by, for example, withholding effort in an attempt to

---

him or her and this profound flaw makes them in some way responsible for the trauma. Accordingly, they inevitably "think, feel, and act in ways that demonstrate the devaluation of themselves," explained Rita Hardiman and Bailey Jackson.

blur the link between poor performance and low ability, making an inference of low ability all the more obscure."

Ultimately, this reaction minimizes "their successes, which gradually erodes their intrinsic motivation to improve performance." Failure and inadequacy, in addition to being anticipated, becomes acceptable. "Failure-accepting students are passive and indifferent to achievement. While they may make sporadic efforts, eventually this gives way to resignation, apathy, and loss of hope." But these are *reactions* (primarily to stigma and negative emotions), not innate or pure indications of something uniquely defective or deficient with Black or poor students, especially those experiencing trauma-based maladaptive neuroplasticity.

"Teachers like to tell students that if they work hard they will succeed—that it is in their control to pay attention, do their homework, and perform well in class. But those assumptions," explained Jim Sporleder, don't necessarily "work for children growing up in high-stress environments," such as those experiencing complex trauma. These students, observed Jensen, "are different because their brains are different. Our brains are designed by nature to reflect the environments they're in"— inclusive of negative race or poverty-based experiences these students may endure repeatedly and in addition to other trauma— "not to 'automatically' rise above them."

These students are generally responded to more conditionally and negatively (as opposed to strategically) in schools by trauma-ignorant educators, effectively reinforcing their underdeveloped capacity to regulate negative emotions and impulsivity in addition to equally underdeveloped levels of academic resilience and self-efficacy coupled with academic underachievement stemming from self-handicapping behavior.

Students experiencing complex trauma rarely consciously "choose to behave differently, but they are faced daily with overwhelming challenges" that untraumatized or lesser traumatized "children never have to confront, and their brains have adapted to

108

suboptimal conditions in ways that undermine good school performance." Their brains have maladapted (i.e., negatively changed) in order to simply survive past and ongoing circumstances, most of which are uncontrollable, negative, and unpredictable (i.e., traumatic).

It's sad to say, but there's typically very little genuine interest, enthusiasm, laughter, empathy, action, determination, and curiosity (i.e., positive emotions) in the learning experience of too many Black and poor (and probably traumatized) students. Conversely, these students tend to experience an abundance of frustration, shame, blame, disgust, anxiety, anger, sadness, apathy, disappointment, hostility, hopelessness, helplessness, and regret (i.e., negative emotions). The unique frequency and intensity of these negative emotions (in addition to the ones experienced outside of the classroom) oftentimes aggravate these students' collective struggle with emotional self-regulation in the classroom or become traumatic stressors themselves.

Emotions, explained Gross, "do not force us to respond in certain ways, they only make it more likely we will do so." Being overexposed to (i.e., chronically experiencing) negative circumstances and emotions oftentimes beyond their control (along with the resulting neuroplasticity) does not somehow validate the negative classroom behaviors committed by far too many Black and poor students.

Recognizing many of these students' overexposure to negative, uncontrollable circumstances and emotions and, even more so, the resulting neuroplasticity does, however, offer us a rational avenue with which to go beyond their current classroom behavior in search of identifying its true (nonstigmatic) origins. Accordingly, it's imperative that when evaluating the presumably innate disruptiveness and deficiencies of Black and poor students, we consistently recall how the human brain, as stated by Jensen, is "designed by nature to reflect the environments they're in, not to 'automatically' rise above them." It's especially imperative to do so if and when the "innateness" of their self-handicapping behavior

109

is semiconsciously being used to justify sustaining negative expectations or not wanting to teach them at all.

Likewise, it should never be minimized (nor used simply as an excuse) just how students experiencing complex trauma "rarely choose to behave differently, but are faced daily with overwhelming challenges" that untraumatized (or lesser traumatized) "children never have to confront, and their brains have adapted to suboptimal conditions" via trauma-based neuroplasticity "in ways that undermine good school performance," specifically their capacity to understand and manage negative emotions.

The "impulsive nature of the body's stress response system," explained Travis Wright, "makes it difficult for traumatized children to regulate their emotions." Consequently, these students can be more susceptible to being angry, domineering, sarcastic, accusatory, defensive, complaining, demanding, depressed, manipulative, rude, dishonest, tactless, intolerant, overemotional, indifferent, frustrated, aggressive, apathetic, disappointed, insensitive, impulsive, hopeless, and/or disrespectful—all of which can trigger disruptive or self-handicapping classroom behavior from students and hasty labeling by educators[23] of these students as (innately) incompetent (i.e., not capable of learning), disinterested in learning, unteachable, or incorrigible.

Because of their struggle to regulate negative classroom emotions and impulsivity, these students typically stop taking enough of the positive academic risks (e.g., giving maximum effort, effectually responding to teacher checks for understanding, adequately studying for assessments, taking advantage of academic supports as needed) required for learning. Their brain tends to uniquely process these risks as most likely becoming shame-inducing experiences based on the perceived psychological threat of anticipated inadequacy and failure. Such experiences, like their previous or ongoing trauma, are expected to somehow overwhelm

---

[23] Hasty labeling made easier by stigma-based expectations.

110

their "capacity to regulate their emotions" and "ability to cope with what they have experienced" and, consequently, become traumatic (or trauma triggers).

"Some of our most stubborn habits," including those that become self-handicapping academic behavior, are fundamentally "products of brain plasticity." Trauma-based maladaptive neuroplasticity is most tangibly manifested in these students' overreliance on self-handicapping academic behavior. As students experiencing complex trauma consistently withdraw from taking academic risks, relying on student-teacher relationships, and other pro-academic behaviors, the neural "circuitry for those activities begins to weaken," noted Doidge. This atrophy is the consequence of neuronal connections not being reinforced via repetition as well as neuroplasticity attributable to experiencing chronic traumatic stress (and continuous cortisol saturation of certain brain areas) in connection with their complex trauma.

They might try sporadically to be "good students," but "their brains will have trouble" with executing those unpracticed pro-academic behaviors, explained Newhouse. Many of these students ultimately "develop something called learned non-use. Learned non-use is not a form of laziness; it is what the brain takes away from repeated efforts to do something, and finding it can't…it will ultimately quit trying" and deploy "its resources in other areas."

Doing so may then cause "harmful habits to become part of learned behavior" as the neural circuitry for some possibly anti-academic behavior begins to strengthen through repetition, especially if using them somehow consistently alleviates preexisting or predicted stress stemming from certain negative academic experiences. Self-handicapping academic behavior usually serve this exact function; it becomes a specific type of trauma-based self-defeating behavior.

Self-handicapping academic behavior includes various "obstacles to successful performance," such as habitually procrastinating, choosing not to participate in an instructional activity (oftentimes accepting the consequences without *seeming* to

111

care), not completing class assignments or homework, giving no or low effort (or demonstrating low-effort syndrome[24]), not adequately studying for assessments, being disruptive or defiant, not paying sufficient attention in class, not effectually responding to teacher checks for understanding, cheating, not taking advantage of academic supports as needed, not reading assigned text, using drugs or alcohol for escapism, failing to get enough sleep to function effectively, placing oneself in a noisy or distracting environment to complete work or study, and quitting regularly.

Not all students experiencing complex trauma demonstrate trauma-based behavior that "undermine good school performance." Some of them, us (the authors of this book) included, "may actually show improvement in school performance," noted Robin Gurwitch and David Schonfeld. "In an attempt to regain a sense of control after trauma, they may become wholly focused on something they can control—schoolwork."

Dan Willingham described self-regulation as the "ability to inhibit the automatic response" (e.g., self-handicapping behavior) and "to do something else; more generally, it refers to the ability to control one's emotions, to control attention and other cognitive processes, and to plan and control behavior in ways that are socially acceptable and help us to achieve our goals."

Much of our ability to self-regulate is observationally learned behavior, primarily from parents and peers. "When emotional regulation is absent, deficient, or poorly matched to situational demands, emotional responses may be excessive, inappropriate, or insufficient," according to Amit Etkin et al. Negative emotions, especially when experienced chronically or traumatically, can lessen our capacity to emotionally self-regulate future negative emotions as a result of maladaptive neuroplasticity.

---

[24] John Ogbu described *low-effort syndrome* as academically unsuccessful students' habit of not being "highly engaged in their schoolwork and homework. The amount of time and effort they invested in academic pursuit is neither adequate or impressive."

Moreover, when there is an excess of negative emotions coupled with a general inability to regulate these negative emotions, (young) people are more likely to act impulsively and disregard the future consequences of self-handicapping behavior. Impulsivity involves behaviors almost exclusively triggered by negative emotions rather than forethought, reflection, goal orientation, or consideration of the consequences. The negative emotions dominant so much of our neuronal resources that our very desire to self-regulate becomes compromised by the urgency of our search for some type of short-term relief from these emotions. Whatever makes us feel a little better in the moment becomes prioritized, even if its self-handicapping or destructive.

In addition to diminishing control over our attitude and behavior, impulsivity directly and negatively impacts academic resilience and self-efficacy. Students who struggle with impulsivity are more likely to quit or self-handicap and, subsequently, become brazenly apathetic or disruptively act out because of negative circumstances that elicit negative emotions like frustration, disappointment, fear (of failure), shame, hopelessness, and helplessness.

This is especially true when knowledge gaps are exposed or their exposure is threatened by the perceived difficulty of a learning activity. Unfortunately, the habitual inclination to quit or self-handicap rather than struggle through the difficulty and accompanying negative emotions ultimately only increases these knowledge gaps as quitting or self-handicapping deprives the student opportunities to practice skills, engage (and eventually comprehend) the new content, and progress from teacher and peer feedback.

Struggling with negative emotions and impulsivity is a human vulnerability, especially for probably traumatized young people, yet oftentimes the stigma of race or poverty colors how educators perceive and respond to the negative classroom behaviors that may result from students engaged in this struggle.

113

Unfortunately, more often than not, Black or poor students experience some type of complex trauma (at least, but usually in addition to, race-based experiences or intergenerational poverty) that inevitably prompts significant maladaptive neuroplasticity. However, these students can also experience *positive neuroplasticity*, especially if we (as trauma-informed educators) want them to, have confidence that they can, and consistently utilize trauma-informed strategies and interventions to make it so. "Brains are designed to respond to experiences," confirmed Jensen, "both good and bad." The brain regions and structures (e.g., the amygdala, hippocampus, prefrontal cortex) negatively changed by chronic traumatic stress can continue to be changed by other external, positive stimuli. "Our neurons are designed by nature to reflect their environment," including a positive (classroom and school) environment.

Our relationships with those students who have experienced complex trauma can create the foundation required for reversing much of the trauma-based maladaptive neuroplasticity they have most likely endured. This can all sound somewhat intimidating at first, but there are several relatively straightforward things we can do every day in our classrooms to develop student-educator trust, demonstrate unconditional positive regard, and plant the trauma-informed seeds of positive neuroplasticity.

The most trauma-informed strategy there is is establishing and maintaining positive educator-student relationships with *all* of our students, even the difficult (and potentially traumatized) ones that most days you really don't feel like having a positive relationship with.   Positive relationships reduce the negative neuroplastic impact of chronic traumatic stress. And while this may also sound like a fairly simple strategy, these relationships, in order to be effective and actually strategic, must feature certain characteristics (e.g., unconditional positive regard, trust, intentional avoidance of trauma triggers) that could be overlooked if not made explicit.

Demonstrating *unconditional positive regard* for each student is arguably the most fundamental commitment an educator must make when establishing trauma-informed relationships with them. Alex Shevrin described unconditional positive regard as "the belief that every student is worthy of care and that worth is not contingent on anything—not compliance with rules, not good behavior, not academic success." This is specifically relevant in educator relationships with students impacted by trauma.

"When our students," particularly those who have experienced trauma, "know we'll care about them no matter what" and we won't suddenly stop caring because of something they say or do, they'll be more apt to take enough of the positive academic risks (e.g., giving maximum effort, effectually responding to teacher checks for understanding, adequately studying for assessments, taking advantage of academic supports as needed) required for learning. Their brains will begin to be less likely to process these risks as probable shame-inducing experiences and less threatened by and anticipatory of inadequacy and failure. Consequently, even traumatized students can change into "good students" as their brains and, consequently, academic behavior, begin to reflect their trauma-informed environment.

Really Don't Think I'm Human[25]
Acknowledging Racial Inequality, Injustice, and Stigma in America as Complex Trauma and Teaching Accordingly

"When you're white in America you're given the freedom to be an individual without the connotations and limitations of your race. In short, you're just a person, instead of a black person. That's an important distinction, and it's one that people who aren't white desperately want to get rid of."

-Frederic Poag

"Among Black Americans, negative psychological responses to racism carry many features associated with trauma."

-Alex L. Pieterse et al.

Racial trauma (i.e., experiencing race, or being Black in America, as a common source of complex trauma) can distinctly impact Black students' ability to succeed academically. Just like children experiencing any other complex trauma, students impacted by racial trauma tend to struggle (because of trauma-based maladaptive neuroplasticity) with regulating negative

---

[25] Excerpted from the following James Baldwin quote from *The Fire Next Time*: "These people have deluded themselves for so long that they really don't think I'm human. I base this on their conduct, not what they say."

emotions and impulsivity as well as overcoming their overreliance on self-handicapping academic behaviors. These students, noted Eric Jensen, rarely consciously "choose to behave differently, but they are faced daily with overwhelming challenges that [White] children never have to confront, and their brains have adapted to suboptimal conditions in ways that undermine good school performance." Yet, most allegedly trauma-informed teachers and administrators have never even heard of the term "racial trauma," including those working in schools with higher percentages of African-American students, so how trauma-informed can they really be?

Merely including the modifier *racial* has nowadays become a "conversational atomic bomb," explained Susan Williams. And "once someone makes the accusation of racism, the dialogue often ends" and the discomfort, defensiveness, and/or denial begins. Or if someone ponders too intelligibly about why, to quote James Loewen, "the sneaking suspicion that African Americans might be inferior still goes unchallenged in the hearts of many blacks and whites." Or agrees too vigorously with Eduardo Bonilla-Silva that "the ultimate goal of the dominant race is to defend its collective interests (i.e., the perpetuation of systemic White privilege)," then that someone (especially if he or she happens to be Black) is somehow deemed divisive or oversensitive or outdated.

However, it's "insufficient insight into the systemic nature of racism," wrote Philomena Essed, that "fuels denial and the generic accusation that black people are oversensitive and resort too quickly to charging racism." Few people wish to be seen or see themselves as racist or beneficiaries or even victims of racism while, nevertheless, racism persists factually and tenaciously. Bonilla-Silva even went so far as to deduce that "racial considerations shade almost everything in America." For all intents and purposes, race (and racial stigma) still operates as the "organizing principle of social relations in itself."

According to Rita Kohli et al., "race is a socially constructed and fluid measure of phenotype that is utilized by whites to

117

differentiate themselves from the 'Other.' Race is used to include and exclude specific groups from equal participation, resources, and opportunity in U.S. society." And "in America," explained Michael Adams, "'race' is fundamentally a white-black issue." Nora Hyland wrote that "the construction of racial categories has played a fundamental role in American history, and Whiteness developed in relationship to particular political and economic forces as a way to create an in-group. The construction of an in-group, or dominant group, necessitates the construction of one or more subordinate out-groups which have been configured in different ways throughout history but have always included people of African descent. Therefore, Whiteness is intimately linked to the subordination and oppression of people of color."

And "instead of being some remnant from the past, the social hierarchy based on race is a critical component in the organization of modern American society." David Wellman wrote that "subordination because of the color of one's skin is a primary determinant of people's position in the social structure. Racism is the structural relationship based on the subordination of one racial group by another. Given this perspective, the determining feature of race relations is not overt prejudice towards blacks, but rather the superior position of whites and the institutions—ideological as well as structural—which maintain it."

Racism has evolved into a constant system of oppression in which the potential of a particular racial group to become fully human is deliberately and fundamentally reduced for the undeniable benefit of another racial group, the latter somehow already being deemed more human. This process of making some people seem less human, this restrictive practice of creating and sustaining stigma, is not always obviously malicious or fully intentional. Oftentimes, it is the result of a handful of people's historical or current decisions or institutional policies that effect embedded, unchallenged sociocultural habits, norms, and paradigms which become an antagonistic structure of forces.

118

Race and racism are far too functional to suddenly become irrelevant or totally implicit. Christopher Bracey agreed that "behaviors that generate and sustain racial inequality in America, though historically conditioned, are not always unconscious or unthinking. To the contrary, such behaviors"—such as White America's collective, reflexive maintenance of social boundaries[26]—are "very much intentional conduct insofar as they are representative of a wholesale acceptance of stereotypes and of conscious indifference to the structural disparity that ensues."

Within systems of oppression such as racism, explained Rita Hardiman et al., "differences are used as an indicator that demarcates those who will benefit from oppression and those who will be targeted by it. An individual will have more or less power, privilege, and access to resources within a system of oppression,

---

[26] Michele Lamont and Virag Molnar defined social boundaries as "objectified forms of social differences manifested in unequal access to and unequal distribution of resources (material and nonmaterial) and social opportunities." Embedded into the sociocultural environment as its status quo, social boundaries establish "identifiable patterns of social exclusion or class and racial segregation." Social boundaries, according to Charles Tilly, "separate 'us' from 'them.'" The social construction of threat (to racial hierarchy and privilege) leads to the social construction of boundaries to somehow minimize that threat. The social group currently with the most social power creates boundaries to reject or contain social groups with less power (yet perceived as threatening) in order to maintain intergroup inequalities.

Michael Schwalbe et al. added that "dominant groups maintain boundaries between subordinate groups to protect their access to resources and maintain their social, economic, and political advantage. These boundaries can be symbolic, interactional, spatial, or all of these. By preserving these boundaries, dominant groups protect the material and cultural capital they have acquired and upon which they rely to preserve their dominance. In plainer terms, the reproduction of inequality depends on elites cooperating to limit Others' access to valued resources."

depending on whether the group to which she or he is perceived to belong to."

"Social equality and privilege," wrote Amos N. Wilson, "across ethno-cultural groups cannot exist simultaneously with White American sociopolitical and economic dominance. The privilege and advantage of this specific ethno-cultural group require the subordination of other groups." Beginning with slavery, "the oppressive configuration White people have assumed in relation to Black people is in good part the result of the fact that we (Black people) have permitted ourselves to remain in a complementary subordinate configuration conducive to their oppressive designs."

Racism even as some awesome, omnipresent oppressive arrangement has remarkably palpable, personal consequences. As brilliantly articulated by Marilyn Frye, the experience of racially "oppressed people is that the living of one's life is confined and shaped by forces and barriers which are not accidental or occasional and hence avoidable, but are systematically related to each other in such a way as to catch one between and among them and restrict or penalize motion in any direction. It is the experience of being caged in."

That distinct experience of being caged in, which can be both psychological and tangible, oftentimes becomes *traumatic*. Chronically, profoundly, and sometimes intensely traumatic.

Complex trauma, according to Robert Carter et al., is "typically interpersonal and generally involves situations in which the person who is traumatized cannot escape from the traumatic experiences because he or she is constrained physically, socially, or psychologically." Racism, concluded Lillian Polanco-Roman et al., "may be better conceptualized as a race-based traumatic stressor"—a type of complex trauma—"rather than as a benign negative experience." To be Black in this country and relatively conscious of just what that implies is to be almost constantly exposed to powerful and dangerous stimuli primed to "overwhelm our capacity to regulate our negative emotions" and "ability to cope with what they have experienced."

Numerous scholars concur that race—or more specifically, racial inequality, injustice, and stigma in America—is a common source of complex trauma. "There are few advantages," observed Kathy Russell, "associated with being Black in America." Racism, noted Jennifer Crocker, "continues to place countless individuals in a position of hopeless discontent." Among Black people in America (children and adolescents included), acknowledged Alex L. Pieterse et al., "negative psychological responses to racism carry many features associated with trauma," specifically complex trauma.

Ongoing exposure to *race-based traumatic stress* is a consistent consequence of simply being Black in America. "Race-based experiences," explained Carter et al., "fall within the domain of traumatic experiences. Racism should be understood as an experience that can produce stress, and that in some cases, the stress can rise to the level of a traumatic stress reaction."

"Some racial and ethnic minority individuals may experience racial discrimination as a psychological trauma, as it may elicit a response comparable to posttraumatic stress." For the experience to be traumatic (i.e., trigger the traumatic stress response), it must somehow be "ambiguous, negative, unpredictable, and/or uncontrollable," which definitely describes most contemporary race-based experiences. "For most people of color," observed Camara Jones, "racism isn't an occasional problem but a subtle, everyday stressor that is added onto all the other stressors in a person's life."

Several recent studies have confirmed that Black people in America tend to experience more trauma than White people, primarily because of our particular exposure to typically negative race-based experiences. Yet, there's a general reluctance, even among Black people, to accept or affirm contemporary racism as a pervasive, ongoing source of complex trauma. We've been collectively somewhat reluctant about acknowledging trauma in general for a variety of reasons, as if we've become convinced that trauma is just for White people. Some of it is access-related, some of it is implicitly not wanting to seem "more defective."[27]

"Real or perceived experiences of racial discrimination," according to Lillian Comas-Díaz et al., including "threats of harm and injury, humiliating and shaming events, and witnessing racial discrimination toward other individuals" can trigger racialized trauma. "Although similar to posttraumatic stress disorder, racial trauma is unique in that it involves ongoing individual and collective injuries due to exposure and reexposure to race-based stress."

"Racism itself may be a traumatic experience." Race-based traumatic stress can be prompted by "experiences involving explicit and obvious racism, racism experienced by loved ones, being vicariously impacted by racist experiences that were learned about, or it can be the result of an accumulation of many small occurrences of subtle forms of racism, such as microaggressions," according to Monnica Williams.

"Racial trauma may involve a negative, sudden, and uncontrollable experience or crisis," confirmed Kenneth Ponds. "Or it may be an ongoing psychological threat that produces feelings of fear, anxiety, depression, and helplessness. Much racial trauma is the result of what are called microaggressions, the everyday verbal or non-verbal slights, snubs, or insults (whether intentional or unintentional) which communicate hostile, derogatory, or negative messages to targeted persons. Microaggressions have a powerful impact upon the psychological well-being of the targeted group or person. Sadly, the most detrimental forms of microaggressions can be delivered by well-

---

[27] According to Erving Goffman, "race is a stigma;" or more specifically, being Black in America is *already* an "undesired differentness. Stigma has traditionally been defined as a sign or a mark that designates the bearer as defective and therefore as meriting less valued treatment than 'normal' people," with "normal" in this regard equated with being White.

122

intentioned individuals who are unaware that they have engaged in harmful conduct toward a socially devalued group."

"Racial trauma is experiencing psychological symptoms such as anxiety, low self-esteem, feelings of humiliation, hypervigilance to threat, sense of a foreshortened future, or lack of hopefulness for your future as a result of repeated exposure to racism or discrimination," explained Erlanger Turner. "There is so much continued racism either directly or indirectly that it's hard to recover from one incident before another occurs." This inability to recover due to chronicity and uncontrollability is largely responsible for race-based experiences becoming traumatic, even though "not every incident of racism will result in racial trauma."

"The trauma of racism refers to the cumulative negative impact of racism on the lives of people of color," observed Dottie Lebron et al., including "significant racial disparities in educational achievement, health, criminal justice system participation, and employment."

Wilson elaborated that "when we look at major American institutions relative to African-Americans, we observe the following: the economic system keeps them poor, the criminal justice system mediates injustice; the educational establishment creates ignorance and intellectual incompetence; the family institution breeds broken homes and 'illegitimate' children; and the health and welfare system catalyzes sickness and administers health-care neglect (the lifespan of African-Americans is actually decreasing)."

"The burden of repetitive and unresolved traumatic experiences associated with racism" and being Black in America, added Lebron et al., "can create severe emotional pain and distress that can overwhelm a person's and community's ability to cope, creating feelings of powerlessness. Cumulatively these unjust experiences," which include everything from slavery, lynching sprees, and Jim Crow laws to educational inequity, residential segregation, and racially biased mass incarceration, "have affected multiple generations."

Shelly Harrell et al. described racism as a "system where power is unevenly distributed along racial lines resulting in the oppression and exclusion of non-White groups." Racism is certainly a unique form of oppression, one based on racial categorization and systemic domination that ultimately designates one racial group superior and the others relatively inferior. Operating deliberately *and* automatically in interpersonal, institutional, and cultural spheres, racial oppression revolves around whatever real or fictitious differences race as a fabricated social category can convince us of.

These differences are then used by the supposedly superior group to explicitly or obscurely justify protracted inequity, exclusion, exploitation, and domination. Racism created and now sustains an oppressive social structure based on racial categorization for the purpose of positioning specific racial groups within existing systems of power and domination. James Loewen wrote that "the most pervasive theme in our history is the domination of black America by white America." And racial oppression is why "in contemporary America," noted Joe Feagin, White people continue to "dominate almost every major organization and most major resources, be they economic, political, educational, or legal."

Conversely, these underlying power relations, even though well-established, continuously negatively (and oftentimes traumatically) impacts "entire target communities," observed Vanissar Tarakali. "For *targets* of oppression," this probable source of complex trauma is "ongoing (it exists over generations and over an individual's entire lifespan); pervasive (it is reinforced by myriad institutions); and traumatizes the targets of oppression through (actual or potential) physical, emotional and spiritual violence, and through the withholding of basic resources necessary to survive and thrive. These collective, pervasive and ongoing ruptures of safety and connection" typically function as complex traumatic stressors.

"Oppression, which is the systemic abuse of power," explained Steven Wineman," intentionally renders certain "people powerless. In turn, powerlessness is the hallmark of traumatic experience. It is therefore inevitable that trauma will be pervasive in a society organized around domination, both because oppression creates countless discrete acts of domination and because institutionalized oppression in itself creates powerlessness and trauma."

"The breadth and depth of domination in our society generates an extraordinary volume of recurring traumatic experience. Virtually everyone routinely runs up against forces on one continuum of oppression or another—individuals in dominant positions, images, written words, institutional arrangements, cultural norms, laws, policies—which demean or degrade or devalue or humiliate or violate or arbitrarily constrain them, and in the face of which they have no sense of efficacy or control. This happens at work, at home, at school, on the streets, in stores, in the media, and in the macro-structures of economic and political power. The result is endless, chronic opportunities for people to experience themselves as victims and to experience trauma."

The eventual realization that you are a permanent member of a social (i.e., racial) group that is "systemically and institutionally treated as inferior—and that your inferior status is constantly reflected and re-enacted in your treatment by members of the dominant group in the course of daily life—creates a psychological reality" powerful and negative enough to typically trigger chronic (race-based) traumatic stress.

Carter et al. defined race-based traumatic stress as a non-White individual's response to isolated or ongoing (and cumulative) experiences of racial inequality, injustice, or stigma as "traumatic or outside of their ability to cope. Some racial and ethnic minority individuals may experience racial discrimination as a psychological trauma, as it may elicit a response comparable to posttraumatic stress" (i.e., trauma-based maladaptive neuroplasticity).

125

"Racial trauma in the lives of Black children and adolescents is rarely, if ever, acknowledged," noted Maryam Jernigan et al., but they are "not excluded from the experiences of racial discrimination. Racism is a reality-based and repetitive trauma in the lives of Black children and adolescents. As such, racial trauma is a viable experience that continues to emerge as a significant concern for this population given its negative psychological consequences," especially its neuroplastic capacity to reduce these young people's ability to regulate negative emotions and impulsivity or overcome their overreliance on self-handicapping academic behaviors.

"By far, the number one stressor for Black people in America is racism. It's not something theoretical or something that disappeared with Jim Crow laws. This is a real and present threat for Black children in America," confirmed Adiaha Spinks-Franklin, and "should be treated as an adverse childhood experience that can also lead to poor academic outcomes. When the brain is under constant threat of a racially motivated experience, it is constantly looking for, assessing, and predicting when the threat may come. That's going to interfere with how well a child performs in school."

As aforementioned, the "ability to self-regulate or modulate emotions is a key predictor of academic success," confirmed Susan Cole et al., largely because this ability ultimately increases academic resilience and prevents overreliance on self-handicapping academic behaviors. Yet, a "lack of capacity for emotional self-regulation," noted Sheree Toth and Dante Cicchetti, "is probably the most striking feature" of students experiencing complex trauma. "Unlike the nontraumatized child, the hypervigilant child cannot shift away from distressing cues in the service of maintaining emotional regulation." This hypervigilance is a consequence of trauma-based maladaptive neuroplasticity.

Students experiencing complex trauma and emotional dysregulation tend to protect their trauma-distorted self-concept

126

from potentially overwhelming negative classroom emotions by overusing self-handicapping academic behaviors. Specifically, these students use self-handicapping behaviors to cope with the potentially traumatic psychological threat of anticipated inadequacy and failure. This anticipation stems from a self-concept already compromised by past or ongoing trauma.

For African-American students, this threat is exaggerated by racial stigma. When students experience the stigma associated with Blackness in America, they concurrently experience the omnipresent, ominous expectation of anticipated inadequacy and failure. Because of stigma, the expectations for Black people are generally negative as well as inadequacy and failure-oriented. Racial inequality is perceived as somehow their fault, a consequence or confirmation of their own inherent inadequacy and individual failure rather than systemic racism.

Hastily labeled by (semiconsciously) stigma-influenced educators as innately incompetent, indifferent, or even incorrigible, many *probably traumatized* Black students are actually "self-worth protective students who struggle with a debilitating fear of failure." In effect, to quote Ted Thompson and Zoe Perry, "their fear of failure is so strong that they will use self-handicapping behaviors such as withholding effort to avoid the risk of failure."

Being "self-protective" is these students' defensive reaction to the perceived inevitably or expectation of inadequacy and failure. They "withhold effort to protect themselves from experiencing failure" and inadequacy. In other words, they avoid academic experiences that potentially generate feelings of failure and inadequacy. However, the academic underdevelopment (i.e., knowledge gaps) that results from avoidance tends to reinforce the initial fear of failure and inadequacy.

Uncertain self-worth is "known to be critical in relation to self-handicapping behaviors. People who are uncertain of their overall self-worth are likely to sabotage their performance intentionally by, for example, withholding effort in an attempt to blur the link between poor performance and low ability, making an inference of low ability all the more obscure."

Ultimately, this reaction minimizes "their successes, which gradually erodes their intrinsic motivation to improve performance." Failure and inadequacy, in addition to being anticipated, becomes acceptable. "Failure-accepting students are passive and indifferent to achievement. While they may make sporadic efforts, eventually this gives way to resignation, apathy, and loss of hope." But these are *reactions* (primarily to stigma and negative emotions), not innate or pure indications of something uniquely defective or deficient with Black students, especially those experiencing racial trauma-based maladaptive neuroplasticity.

"Teachers like to tell students that if they work hard they will succeed—that it is in their control to pay attention, do their homework, and perform well in class. But those assumptions," explained Jim Sporleder, don't necessarily "work for children growing up in high-stress environments," such as those experiencing racial trauma. These students, observed Jensen, "are different because their brains are different. Our brains are designed by nature to reflect the environments they're in"— inclusive of negative race-based experiences these students may endure repeatedly and in addition to other trauma—"not to 'automatically' rise above them."

Yet, these students are generally responded to more conditionally and negatively (as opposed to strategically) in schools by educators unwilling or (in most cases) unable to associate their negative academic behavior with experiencing racial trauma and trauma-based neuroplasticity. And most discussions about the impact of race in the classroom (in general, not necessarily those incorporating the probability of racial trauma) are quickly dismissed as somehow manufacturing excuses, justifying negative academic behavior, or lowering expectations for underperforming Black students.

Children and adolescents are actually more vulnerable to race-based traumatic stress than adults, primarily because the sense of uncontrollability attached to racial trauma can be more overwhelming to nonadults naturally not as proficient or confident in their capacity to control external circumstances (e.g., to stop the traumatic experience) or their internal response to those circumstances (e.g., cope with the experience before it becomes traumatic). This sense of uncontrollability can ultimately trigger a greater, more incessant traumatic stress response (and trauma-based maladaptive neuroplasticity) than the traumatic experiences themselves.

Exposure to the traumatic stress of uncontrollability causes an accelerated loss of PFC size and function and increase in amygdala size and function relative to "normal" traumatic stress. According to Avis Hains et al., "when we feel stressed and out of control, high levels of norepinephrine and dopamine release rapidly weaken PFC, while strengthening more primitive emotional responses and habits mediated by the amygdala."

Chronic exposure to the stress of uncontrollability induces greater "loss of PFC pyramidal cell spines and atrophy of dendrites…PFC gray matter decreases and PFC connectivity" weakens quickly. "This can save our lives when we are in danger and rapid, reflexive responding is needed, but can be detrimental when more thoughtful solutions are needed," such as those associated with a child's "capacity to regulate their emotions" and "ability to cope with what they have experienced." This compromised capacity to regulate and ability to cope significantly increases a child or adolescent's vulnerability to race-based experiences repetitively triggering traumatic stress and additional, aggravated maladaptive neuroplasticity.

A greater sense of sustained controllability increases the prefrontal cortex's ability to regulate and calm the amygdala, specifically as it relates to our perception of traumatic experiences. Uncontrollability, particularly when persistent, decreases that ability and, consequently, makes the amygdala far more active than necessary. More cortisol is released, eventually leading to prolonged cortisol saturation in certain brain areas.

Constant cortisol saturation, as aforementioned, significantly changes neural structures like the hippocampus and prefrontal cortex (PFC), both of which are gradually reduced in size and activity as cortisol annihilates hippocampus and PFC neurons via prolonged overactivation. Conversely, continuous cortisol production increases the size and activity of the amygdala. The now hyperactive and hypertrophied amygdala promotes persistent states of hypervigilance and heightened emotional reactivity, even our traumatic stress response is exacerbated.

Neuroscientific studies have confirmed these brain changes can be triggered via direct race-based experiences as well as indirect, vicarious, or even intergenerational exposure to racial trauma. "For children who witness racial trauma indirectly or vicariously," explained Jernigan et al., "the impact can be equally distressing. Inherent in the conceptualization of racial trauma is the deliberate targeting of persons of color because of their racial background. Consequently, when Black youths observe peers' experiences of racism, they may begin to wonder if they will be targeted next."

Increasing their unique vulnerability is the unfortunate reality that the very "process by which Black children have formulated their identities" and self-concept, observed Aza Nedhari, is largely "rooted in trauma."

According to Jernigan et al., "Black youths are subjected to indirect racial socialization processes, which in American society historically are negative for persons of color. Such experiences impact the internalization of messages about what it may mean to identify with a particular racial group. Racial socialization includes specific messages and practices that provide information about personal and group identity; intergroup and interindividual relationships; and positions in the social hierarchy."

Black children and adolescents are typically socialized about race in ways that prevent them from developing an authentically

130

positive self-concept or resilient optimism with regard to being Black in America. While "no presumption of inferiority attaches to whiteness in our culture," as noted by Robin Lenhardt, it has long been normative American behavior to believe—at least semiconsciously—that "innate inferiority correlates with dark skin color." Although it's hardly ever displayed publicly or spoken aloud, it's constantly implied in subtle interpersonal interactions, consistent injustices, and stubborn institutional inequities that, to cite James Baldwin, "being Black is a terrible thing to be."

Attributable to America's peculiar racial history and culture, there are powerful negative connotations associated within being Black in this country. Possessing this particular trait oftentimes comes with a persistent feeling of somehow being flawed and inadequate, or to quote Marilyn Sorenson, "of *being* something wrong." This feeling can become so fixed and normal that we lose awareness of its existence and stigmatic origins.

Conversely, White people in America, explained Allan Johnson, "have the privilege of being able to assume acceptance as 'normal' members of society...living in a world full of cultural images that confer a sense of legitimacy and social desirability." Being White in America, Feagin added, "means rarely or never having to think about it. Whiteness is the national norm, and thus the white majority's views, practices, and culture are generally seen as normal" and positive.

Blackness (or being Black) is not naturally stigmatizing (i.e., indicative of somehow being "less human"); in fact, stigma itself is as an artificial, socially fabricated construct. Susan Fiske detailed how "years, even generations, of explicit and implicit cultural messages—gleaned from parents, the media, first-hand experiences, and countless other sources—link particular physical appearances with a host of traits, positive or negative." These messages are an inherent part of the American socialization process. "The roots of these messages can stretch back centuries" and has "origins in the age of slavery."

131

The stigma of Blackness in America originated in the need to suddenly justify the wholesale enslavement or murder (in the process or perpetuation of enslavement) of Black people associated the Transatlantic Slave Trade. According to Michael Bradley, "the economics of slavery required and invented a doctrine of differing racial potential." The enslaved African's "different physical appearance provided a convenient peg upon which to hang the argument that this represented the external sign of more profound ineradicable mental and moral inferiorities. It was an easily grasped mode of reasoning, and in this way the obvious difference in their social status was equated with their obviously different physical appearance, which, in turn, was taken to indicate a fundamental biological difference. What had only been a social difference was now transformed into a biological difference which would serve, it was hoped, to justify and maintain the social difference."

Carolyn Martindale agreed that racial stigma and "negative stereotypes of African Americans have been deeply ingrained in American culture ever since Africans were first brought to this country in chains." The norms, images, and messages within American culture have consistently and continue to affirmed the "assumed superiority of white people and the assumed inferiority of people of color," noted Beverly Tatum.

"From childhood we are inundated with images that convey racial inequality in American society," explained Lincoln Quillian. "The images originate from the media and our personal observations, and both represent actual inequality and construct a view of that inequality that includes stereotypical distortions." We began to make certain cognitive associations related to the more consistent aspects of this inequality, like expecting Black people to be unintelligent, lazy, unimportant, inferior, or incomplete (simply because they are Black), and that completeness somehow equates to Whiteness.

Research recently completed by Patricia Devine and Andrew Elliot confirmed that the typical American brain, regardless of its

132

owner's racial affiliation, tends to change to reflexively associate negative, inferiority-related stereotypes with Black people. Simply existing in the racial stigma-laden culture of America maintains our brain's vulnerability to eventually encoding racist, anti-Black stereotypes, which are "broadcasted or implied by the news media, magazines, institutions, television, newspapers, books, and every other medium you can think of," observed Stanley Williams.

Even Black students from high-income household are not immune from this traumatic racial socialization processes, which could explain why so many of them also tend to struggle (albeit to a lesser degree) with regulating negative emotions and impulsivity as well as overcoming their overreliance on self-handicapping academic behaviors.

The tangible consequences of being Black in America, the "lived experience of race," to cite Brian Smedley et al., "or to be more blunt, racism, influences how people are treated, what resources and jobs are available to them, where they are likely to live, how they perceive the world, what environmental exposures they face, and what chances they have to reach their full potential. Educational, housing and wealth-accumulating opportunities have been shaped by a long history of racism" and continues to be significantly (and oftentimes explicitly) racially determined and potentially traumatic.

Bracey specified that "African-Americans with the same level of education as whites continue to earn substantially less. Blacks continue to occupy proportionally fewer managerial positions and proportionally greater service and unskilled labor positions. Median family income for African Americans is roughly two-thirds that of whites. Black youth continue to lag behind whites in performance on standardized tests for mathematics and reading comprehension. The percentage of African-American children under the age of eighteen who live in poverty is almost double that of whites. The same is true for the number of births to unwed mothers. Homicide victimization rates for blacks are nearly double the rates for whites. Incarceration rates for black men are seven

133

times those of white men. African-American adult men and women have a shorter life expectancy than their white counterparts; with black infant mortality rates approximately double those for whites."

"Each of us is perhaps familiar with one or two of these points of comparison, and it is easy to remain relatively unfazed by evidence of disparity in an isolated aspect of social life. Yet it is more difficult to remain unmoved when confronted by the totality of racial disparity presented here. The collected data create a mosaic image of a racial caste, and as such demand our full attention. It immediately calls into question banalities such as 'the civil rights era ended racial discrimination' or 'we live in a color-blind society.' More importantly, it gives force to the claim that nearly every aspect of our lives is mediated by race."

"Historically," explained E. Yvonne Moss and Wornie Reed, the "status of blacks relative to whites has been one of subordination; race has been a primary factor in determining social stratification. Despite improvements in various aspects of American life, racial stratification has not changed in any fundamental sense." Yet, "public policies tend to treat this racial inequality as a product of poor personal decision-making," observed Kate Shuster, "rather than acknowledging it as the result of racialized systems and structures that restrict choice and limit opportunity."

Beginning at an early age, "negative stereotyping conjoined with the imposition of negative residential, occupational, social, educational, experiential circumstances on Black people," noted Wilson, foster a persistent sense of threat typically perceived as "ambiguous, negative, unpredictable, and/or uncontrollable" (i.e., traumatic). The multiple and persistent ways in which experienced, perceived, or anticipated racial injustice, inequity, or stigma (as threatening external stimuli) affect Black people in America oftentimes becomes traumatizing.

Ingrid Waldron et al. added that "when looking at the broader societal structures, it is important to acknowledge the health and mental health impact of racism as a product of structural racism that operates through the laws, norms and rules of governance at the societal level, institutional racism that is embedded in the processes and practices of organizational structures, and 'everyday discrimination' that is expressed in interpersonal relations and daily interactions between individuals. Taken together, these experiences put racialized groups," particularly Black people, at a greater risk for chronic traumatic stress.

Racism may still function as a traumatic catalyst, according to Janet Helms et al., "even when there is no recent evidence of threat to life" and may operate as an "exacerbating stressor" to "commonly referenced traumatic situations" (e.g., emotional, sexual, or physical abuse; witnessing domestic violence; parental neglect or abandonment; homelessness or residential instability). Racism prompts recurring "race-based threats to one's emotional and psychological well-being," which can be "sudden or systemic, intentional or not, vague and ambiguous, direct and specific, or vicarious. Regardless of the form racism takes, racist incidents are, at minimum, a form of emotional abuse and, therefore, can be traumatic."

Because it is generally experienced as continuous or repetitive trauma, *everyday racism* in particular should be appreciated as a highly probable source for chronic race-based traumatic stress. According to Polanco-Roman et al., the subtle racist attitudes and actions unremarkably permeating daily life in American society "may yield emotional and psychological injury that negatively impacts mental health through eliciting traumatic stress, as they are often perceived as negative, unexpected, ambiguous, repeated, and out of the individual's control."

Essed described everyday racism as "the integration of racism into everyday situations through practices (cognitive and behavioral) that activate underlying power relations." Everyday racism is more so a systemic than individual-based "process involving the continuous, often unconscious, exercise of power predicated in taking for granted the privileging of whiteness."

Non-white Americans are subtly victimized mostly by "systematic, recurrent, and familiar practices on an everyday basis" rather than "extreme incidents."

Although it is oftentimes interpersonal, everyday racism is "distinct from the individual racism of racist individuals and instead reveals the systemic qualities of a racist society," which feature "structural inequalities reinforced through everyday practices and interactions that maintain the social oppression of racial minorities."

Everyday racism can be enacted individually (i.e., interpersonally) and is embedded in each of our core institutions, including economics, media, education, and government. "Everyday racism is a process of problematization, marginalization, and containment. Racism puts mechanisms in place that declares black people (or any outgroup) to be a problem, marginalizes them through ethnocentrism and barriers to participation, and contains them through forms of suppression such as intimidation, pacification, and majority rule."

However, the most "crucial characteristic of everyday racism is that it concerns mundane practices." It centers on "injustices recurring so often that they are almost taken for granted—nagging, annoying, debilitating, seemingly small injustices one comes to expect," but may not ever expect to be traumatic. "Everyday racism, though felt persistently, is often difficult to pinpoint. Microinjustices become normal, fused into familiar practices, practices taken for granted, attitudes and behaviors sustaining racial injustice. Continuous disrespect and hostilities nurture alienation from society, or even from self."

"Events experienced as negative, out of one's control, sudden, ambiguous, and repeated increase an individual's stress response," noted Carter et al. Accordingly, "these events deepen emotional pain and can lead to traumatic responses, including hypervigilance, avoidance or numbing and emotional distress." Experiences can be "traumatic because they are emotionally painful," explained Eve Carlson, or "because they involve the threat of emotional pain.

136

In this case the negative valence is related to the psychological meaning of the event to the individual, not the physical consequences of the event."

The constant psychological threat of the next negative race-based experience, and the inevitable feeling of being powerless to stop this threat because it is so persistent, could trigger a traumatic response, most likely hypervigilance. Hypervigilance is used unconsciously as a defensive mechanism. However, hypervigilance, particularly when chronic, is both a catalyst for and consequence of trauma-based maladaptive neuroplasticity. The hypervigilant amygdala is constantly activating the stress response, which triggers the overproduction of cortisol, eventually leading to prolonged cortisol saturation in certain brain areas. Continuous hypervigilance changes our brain and as it changes our brain, the now hyperactive and hypertrophied amygdala promotes even more persistent states of hypervigilance and heightened emotional reactivity.

Consequently, students experiencing racial trauma as complex trauma, explained Ray Wolpow et al., are "often operating within the mode of 'survival in the moment.' Survival in the moment," even when the moment occurs during class, is governed by hyperactive, cortisol-saturated "pathways in the brain that appraise threat, sacrifice context for speed of response, make decisions outside of consciousness, and mobilize the body for fight, flight, or freeze."

These students are therefore remarkably more inclined to emotionally overreact to (be triggered by) a current action or circumstance that somehow reminds them of past or ongoing trauma as if it could become current trauma. As opposed to critical thought or constructive coping mechanisms, fear of not psychologically surviving in the moment is prioritized and responses like impulsivity, emotional dysregulation, and self-handicapping behaviors are normalized as supposed survival techniques.

Their brain, concluded Mary Flannery, "is changed by repeated traumatic experiences" and this chronic triggering (or retraumatization). "The result is a brain that has structurally adapted" for psychological "survival under the most stressful circumstances—but not for success in school."

Complex trauma "interferes with being fully present with a 'learning-ready' brain," explained Christopher Blodgett. Complex trauma can "impair the development of children's ability to regulate their emotions and to control impulsive behaviors," confirmed Cole et al. "Reactions can be triggered in hypervigilant children if they feel they are being provoked or if something reminds them of the trauma. An incident or remark that might seem minor to a nontraumatized child may be perceived as threatening by a traumatized child, who then responds in a seemingly disproportionate way. It is helpful for teachers to know what triggers might cause a traumatized child to become hyperaroused or to reexperience a traumatic event in the classroom."

Carter et al. explained that it seems reasonable to conclude that everyday racism "can be a traumatic stressor," (i.e., a traumatic experience or situation that overwhelms our perceived ability/resources to cope). Traumatic experiences such as everyday racism typically trigger the traumatic stress response repeatedly since our survival (or at least quality of life) may be compromised on a daily basis beyond our perceived ability/resources to cope with the threat. Much of the trauma associated with everyday racism is "related to the perception of a racist event as emotionally painful (negative), sudden, and out of one's control, criteria that are consistent with the traditional definition of trauma."

"Race-based traumatic stress," according to Thema Bryant-Davis and Carlota Ocampo, "can be defined as (a) an emotional injury that is motivated by hate or fear of a person or group of people as a result of their race; (b) a racially motivated stressor that overwhelms a person's capacity to cope; (c) a racially motivated,

138

interpersonal severe stressor that causes bodily harm or threatens one's life integrity; or (d) a severe interpersonal or institutional stressor motivated by racism that causes fear, helplessness, or horror."

Everyday racism, with its plethora of intergroup and interpersonal racial *microstressors* (e.g., microaggressions, microinequities, microinsults, microinvalidations, and microassaults), can easily satisfy any of these specific standards.

"Racist incidents perpetrated at the individual level by an overtly racist perpetrator that involve verbal, physical, or some other type of abuse or assault fit the standard definition of trauma. In fact, these incidents would be traumatic regardless of the motivation (racist or otherwise). However, viewing racist incidents through the narrow lens of overt, individual racism" conceals, even from the supposedly trauma-informed, the traumatic impact of everyday racism and its cache of covert microstressors on so many Black students.

"Overt racism has largely been replaced with more covert, subtle, ambiguous, and complex racist incidents that operate at institutional and cultural levels. These forms of racism are confusing because they are among the structures that maintain the status quo in our society. Covert racist incidents form the social backdrop against which racially marginalized people must function day to day. The incidents are never far from one's consciousness and require expenditures of cognitive energy, hypervigilance, and coping. Thus, when an experience of overt racism occurs or even an experience of ambiguous racism, the experience simply jumps out of the social fabric that already encapsulates us, and we are primed for a traumatic response."

Researchers using fMRI demonstrated that there is no significant difference in how the human brain reacts to covert and overt racist stimuli. Hypothetically, their potential to trigger trauma is equal. However, most "potentially traumatic racist incidents are nonphysical and/or covert." Their traumatic effect is largely associated with repetitive and cumulative exposure to

139

psychologically threatening, everyday racist experiences and microstressors over time.

"The repetitive nature of the incidents can make the experience traumatic. One incident alone may not be traumatizing, but multiple microaggressions can build to create an intense traumatic impact."

Glenn Miller explained that trauma traditionally "involves a singular, unexpected event of catastrophic magnitude." Yet, "for African-Americans, racism is never a single act. It is expectable and persistent." Everyday racism can theoretically occur *every day*. "Almost all interracial encounters are prone to microaggressions" and other microstressors, noted Derald Sue et al. The cumulative impact of everyday racism from childhood to adulthood is probably traumatic on some level for *most* African-Americans.

White Americans tend to deny, disregard, or become defensive about their role in and the daily reality of racial microstressors (as well as everyday racism in general). They generally argue (even if they don't fully believe) that "minorities are doing better in life, that discrimination is on the decline, that racism is no longer a significant factor in the lives of people of color, and that equality has been achieved. More important, the majority of Whites do not view themselves as racist or capable of racist behavior," especially White teachers with mostly Black students.

Conversely, African-Americans of all ages generally notice everyday racism (even if we don't articulate it as such), perceiving "Whites as (a) racially insensitive, (b) unwilling to share their position and wealth, (c) believing they are superior, (d) needing to control everything, and (e) treating them poorly because of their race. People of color believe these attributes are reenacted every day in their interpersonal interactions with Whites, oftentimes in the form of microaggressions. While hate crimes receive the most attention, the greatest damage to the life experiences of people of color is from racial microaggressions."

Debra Roberts and Sherry Molock maintained that the most "dangerous thing about microaggressions is while they may be small intentional or unintentional offenses, they can accumulate and become burdensome over time for those who experience them. One of the most insidious features of microaggressions is that sometimes they are hard to confront because they are so subtle" and ambiguous; ambiguity usually increases the trauma potential of a negative, race-based experience. "Because they tend to involve small incidences or indirect insults, it is easy for the perpetrators of microaggressions to dismiss or negate your perception that the behavior or comment was racist. After a while, you may begin to question whether you are being overly sensitive."

Black youth experience racial microaggressions as often as (if not more than) Black adults. They are subjected to microaggressions (and other microstressors) from society in general as well as those committed by their oftentimes White teachers and administrators.

David Zhou described microaggressions as indirect interracial "interactions that convey hostile language. Or, subtle expressions of what some would call bigotry or prejudice that express power in a social setting."

Anderson J. Franklin agreed that microaggressions are "subtle acts or attitudes that are experienced as hostile, and that fit a history and pattern of personal racial slights and disregard. They act as status reminders by their implicit suggestion of our unworthiness. They convey a 'Stay in your place' message. A life history of microaggressions would make anyone extremely vigilant about personal dignity and self-respect...perpetual vigilance is stressful and tips some people toward counterproductive and dysfunctional behavior" (e.g., emotional dysregulation, impulsivity, and self-handicapping academic behavior).

Microaggressions create *insidious exposure*, which Carter et al. described as "both chronic and pervasive exposure to racism. Over time subjective experience of repetitive and cumulative

141

exposure could be traumatically impactful. Such insidious exposure can reinforce assumptions that the world and life are unfair to people of particular races, that the dominant White race is at best unconcerned and at worst malevolent, and Black life has little positive worth and meaning."

"The events that may produce race-based traumatic stress reaction(s) over time occur in many different forms. Racial encounters may be direct or subtle and ambiguous. They can occur on an interpersonal level (microaggressions, verbal assaults, use of symbols or coded language), can be the effect of structural or systemic acts," or it can occur through "actions that involve treating a person on the basis of a stereotype or as if he or she, a unique person, is invisible. These acts can produce a form of trauma or race-based traumatic stress."

"Race-based events that may be severe or moderate, and daily slights or microaggressions, can produce psychological harm or injury when they have memorable impact or lasting effect or through cumulative or chronic exposure to the various types or classes of racism. The most severe forms may not be physical attacks, but rather more subtle acts. The severity of a race-based event should be determined by the strength and intensity of the person's reaction and the symptom cluster that emerges. Because many aspects of racism can occur throughout one's life, severity may be a consequence of the cumulative effects of numerous events. For example, one seemingly innocuous or minor event could be the last straw in a series of accumulated racial incidents, causing a person to feel that he or she can no longer manage the stress and pain of encounters with racism. One may be stressed, but the level of stress may not reach the threshold for being traumatic until the trigger or last straw."

Sue et al. described racial microaggressions as "brief and commonplace daily verbal, behavioral, or environmental slights, insults, indignities and denigrating messages, whether intentional or unintentional, that communicate hostile, derogatory, or negative racial slights and insults towards people of color. Studies support

142

the fact that people of color frequently experience microaggressions, that they are a continuing reality in their day-to-day interactions" and result "in a negative racial climate and emotions of self-doubt, frustration, and isolation on the part of victims."

"Microaggressions are often unconsciously delivered in the form of subtle snubs or dismissive looks, gestures, and tones. These exchanges are so pervasive and automatic in daily conversations that they are often dismissed and glossed over as being innocent and innocuous. They are, nevertheless, detrimental to persons of color because microaggressions impair performance in the workplace, in the classroom, and in a multitude of other settings by sapping the psychic and spiritual energy of recipients and by creating inequities."

Racial microaggressions can cause chronic, potentially traumatic stress for Black (and other non-White) people through their inherently "denigrating messages: 'You do not belong,' 'You are abnormal,' 'You are intellectually inferior,' 'You cannot be trusted,' and 'You are all the same.' Feelings of powerlessness, invisibility, forced compliance and loss of integrity, and pressure to represent one's group are some of the consequences."

Racism must not be "objectively defined to produce a traumatic response in a victim," acknowledged Bryant-Davis and Ocampo. "If the victim perceives the event as potentially racist, a traumatic response may occur." In other words, *merely perceiving* a highly negative experience as racist or race-based could trigger racial trauma, regardless of the accuracy of the perception. Nicole Jagusztyn noted that "as long as a person feels they are subject to differential treatment based on group membership, this perception may have adverse effects."

The "perception of an environmental stimulus as racist" can result in a traumatic stress response. "There is a tendency to discount perceptions of racism as stressful" and potentially traumatic, observed Rodney Clark et al., yet "this denial is inconsistent with the stress literature, which highlights the importance of the appraisal process. The perception of (environmental) demands as stressful is more important in initiating stress responses" than the actuality.

"Given that psychological and physiological stress responses are more sensitive to an individual's perception of stressfulness than objective demands, there is no a priori way of determining if an environmental stimulus will be perceived as racist by an individual." All racism is perceived, if you want to get technical. "The individual who experiences racism does so as a result of their subjective perception of the actions of others." Accordingly, "the initiation of psychological stress responses as a result of perceiving environmental stimuli involving racism would qualify race-based stimuli as stressors" that could certainly reach the threshold for being traumatic.

"Numerous psychological stress responses may follow perceptions of racism. These responses include anger, paranoia, anxiety, hopelessness-helplessness, frustration, resentment, and fear." At some point early in life Black people began to anticipate racism. "Merely the anticipation of racism," Jason Silverstein explained, "and not necessarily the act," is enough to trigger a traumatic stress response. "Just the fear of racism alone should switch on the body's stress-response systems. This makes sense— if we think our environment contains threats, then we will be on guard."

"For the most part," wrote Lenhardt, "racially stigmatized individuals have relatively few places where they can go and be assured of not being exposed to racist or racialized conduct or remarks. This reality may leave stigmatized individuals feeling that they must be constantly 'on' and vigilant against racialized conduct. It may also have psychological consequences, leaving them feeling somewhat insecure or uncertain in their social interactions with others." These consequences include, to cite Devika Choudhuri et al., "feeling powerless, invisible, and less valid than Whites and pressure to represent his/her racial group in such a way as to not promote stereotyping."

Elizabeth Pascoe and Laura Richman added that "if an individual perceives discrimination on a regular basis, these stress responses should be activated more often, potentially leading to a consistently negative emotional state. Chronic, heightened physiological stress responses, such as cardiovascular reactivity and cortisol responses, are also included in this pathway. Experiences of perceived discrimination may contribute to health problems through allostatic load developed by heightened stress responses and negative emotional states."

With everyday racism, racist thought, emotional reaction, and behavior are typically more ambiguous and, as a result, necessarily more perceptual than explicit, which may result in a far more chronic, potentially traumatic stress response than African-Americans experienced historically.

Sue et al. explained that African-Americans must "rely heavily on experiential reality that is contextual in nature and involves life experiences from a variety of situations." We begin to identify (and accumulate as emotional memories) anticipatory cues in our lived experience with (everyday) racism. Because of this lived experience and the pervasiveness of verifiable racism, individual incidents of perceived racism oftentimes become perceived as "nonrandom events" with "the only similarity 'connecting the dots' to each and every one of these incidents being the color of our skin."

Conversely, "most White Americans do not share these multiple experiences, and they evaluate their own behaviors in the moment through a singular event. Thus, they fail to see a pattern of bias, are defended by a belief in their own morality, and can in good conscience deny that they discriminated." In other words, they tend to not perceive racism as consistently as African-Americans, even when the possibly ambiguous thought, emotional reaction, and behavior is *actually* racist.

We also believe that racial stigma is regularly experienced as complex trauma by Black students across this country.

Carol Miller and Cheryl Kaiser confirmed that not only can "stigma be a source of chronic stress for stigmatized people," it can ultimately become a complex traumatic stressor specifically because stigma is highly uncontrollable[28] and experienced as a "repeated instance of the same type of trauma over a period of time" or in addition to other types of traumatic stressors. Complex trauma involves recurring, prolonged, or cumulative exposure to trauma-inducing situations; stigma can certainly be (or prompt) such a situation.

Justin Powell described stigma as a "socially constructed, negatively valued differentness." Erving Goffman defined stigma as "as a sign or a mark that designates the bearer as defective and therefore as meriting less valued treatment than 'normal' people." In fact, the stigmatized are typically "viewed as less than fully human" because of their possession of this socially defined and disfavored attribute. "Stigma is the situation of the individual who is disqualified from full social acceptance" and "reduced in our minds from a whole and usual person to a tainted, discounted one."

In America, "race is a stigma." Specifically, being Black in America remains to this day an "undesired differentness" that "conveys a negative social identity." Race creates a stigma that, to quote Caroline Howarth, "produces and sustains material

---

[28]   As noted by Gregory Herek, "stigma is not inherent in a particular trait or membership in a particular group; rather, society collectively identifies particular characteristics or groups, and assigns negative meaning and value to some of them, thereby 'constructing' stigma."

For instance, racial stigma, explained Robin Lenhardt, "like race itself—is ultimately a social construct. This means that the norms and rules about which categories of individuals will be valued or devalued are defined by society, even by the government, but not by nature. There is, after all, nothing inherently wrong with having dark skin or being a racial minority in society. Such a status does not itself lead to mistreatment or discrimination. An attribute that stigmatizes one type of possessor can confirm the usualness of another, and therefore is neither creditable nor discreditable as a thing in itself. An attribute becomes disfavored only because of the social information it carries."

inequalities and is anchored in histories of domination, prejudice, exclusion, and poverty."

Glenn Loury described how an "awareness of the racial 'otherness' of blacks is embedded in the social consciousness of the American nation owing to the historical fact of slavery and its aftermath. This inherited stigma even today exerts an inhibiting effect on the extent to which African-Americans can realize their full human potential. Fundamental to the processes of race-making in the United States have been the institution of chattel slavery and the associated rituals and customs that supported the master-slave hierarchy and dishonored the slave. In the experience of the United States, slavery was a thoroughly racial institution. Therefore, the social meaning of race that emerged in American political culture was closely connected with the dishonorable status of enslavement."

The cognitive processes still "linked to racial stigma and the negative meanings it conveys distort social relationships," noted Robin Lenhardt, "obscure the salience of racial disparities, and lead to conscious and unconscious behavior on the part of nonstigmatized individuals that intensifies racial disadvantage. In the end, they operate to reify existing racial hierarchies and lock African Americans and other racial minorities into a permanent 'outsider' status—even where laws and policies require formal equality among the races."

"Part of the strength of the 'societal devaluations' associated with race in this country is that 'they cannot be dismissed as the ravings of some idiosyncratic bigot.' They are shared and consensual, which means that they cannot easily be ignored. This, perhaps even more than the precise character of the messages conveyed about race, is what makes racial stigma such a powerful social force."

Stigma creates a "hierarchical separation of human worth," explained Joe Pettit. "Stigma creates an 'Us vs. Them' sorting of human beings" that implies the inferior status, negative regard, displaced blame, and relative social powerlessness of members of

147

the "them" group. Stigma enables the aforementioned negative outcomes associated with racial inequality to be "blamed either exclusively or primarily on the life choices of individual black people."

"What is it about so many black people that causes them to make choices with such negative outcomes? The answer is unavoidable. Some kind of flaw must be thought to exist in these individuals that causes them persistently to make so many bad choices over time. However flawed white people may be, then, their flaws are not such as to produce negative outcomes at the rate that appears among blacks. Collectively speaking then, whites must be understood as superior to blacks."

One of the most fundamental sociocultural norms of America is that all people (i.e., social groups) are *not equal*. Via stigma, "our society assigns value to groups of people," explained Gail Christopher. "It is a process that is embedded in the consciousness of Americans and impacted by centuries of bias" and tangible inequity. However, this entire process has practically become imperceptible because it's so outrageously normalized. Yet, "by the time children are in kindergarten," noted by Sylvia Law, most are aware of racial stigma, and largely due to stigma "both White and Black children attach positive value to Whiteness and negative value to Blackness."

Racial stigma remains a chronically negative sociopsychological experience responsible for a variety of aversive reactions from those subjected to it. Research shows that recurring experiences of racial stigma, either directly or vicariously, cause stigma, shame, anxiety, anger, aggression, apathy, inequality, injustice, illness, despair, docility, self-handicapping behavior, stereotypic behavior, learned helplessness, and, perhaps most impactfully, complex traumatic stress. "Because stigma conveys a devalued social identity within a particular context," explained Mark Hatzenbuehler et al., "it creates unique stressors."

The stigmatized cannot control being stigmatized; if they could, they'd instantly stop being stigmatized or possessing the

148

stigma (e.g., stop being Black). "Society," explained Gregory Herek, "collectively identifies particular characteristics or groups, and assigns negative meaning and value to some of them, thereby 'constructing' stigma." Stigma isn't constructed organically, arbitrarily, or benignly. Whatever characteristics or social groups that a society decides to negatively value are selected because it "consequently disadvantages, devalues, and disempowers those who have it."

The uncontrollability of stigma enhances its capacity to function as a complex trauma. Adding uncontrollability to an ongoing, potentially traumatic experience can make it even more overwhelming, especially to children and adolescents naturally not yet proficient or confident in their capacity to control external circumstances or their internal response to those circumstances. The more overwhelming the experience—with regard to our capacity to regulate our emotions and cope with what we have experienced—the more likely we will respond to the experience as complex trauma. Uncontrollability can ultimately trigger a greater, more incessant traumatic stress response (and trauma-based maladaptive neuroplasticity) than the traumatic experience of stigma itself.

Lenhardt observed how "just as stigmatizers begin to learn negative attitudes about and certain affective responses to racially stigmatized individuals in infancy, the stigmatized begin to internalize normative judgments about their race very early in their lives, learning such judgments, in some cases, from their own parents as well as from others. Almost from the beginning, they are in a constant battle to reconcile their actual selves with the virtual identities imposed by the steady barrage of negative images coming from the media and other sources. Even where negative stereotypes about race are expressly rejected, mere awareness of them may leave racially stigmatized individuals feeling at a very deep—perhaps even unconscious—level that their attribute may warrant some of the adverse treatment their racial group incurs."

Racial stigma is learned through socialization and *felt* throughout life. Felt stigma, according to Elizabeth Pinel and Jennifer Bosson, "presupposes a sense of stigma consciousness, which is a state of self-consciousness in which people with a stigmatized condition sense subtle or overt negative treatment by others" and have "an expectation of being judged on the basis of one's group membership, irrespective of one's actual behavior." And sadly, you can't just suddenly stop feeling stigma.

Additionally, Jonathan Cook et al. noted that "people with visible stigmas (such as African Americans) are thought to incorporate their stigma into self-identity more centrally than those with potentially concealable stigmas (such as being gay), largely because the stigma is an unavoidable feature of any social interaction."

Racial stigma is a *social evaluative threat*, which means it attacks our self-concept or social value (i.e., our social self). According to new neuroscientific evidence, social evaluative threats trigger the kind of traumatic stress that has the greatest neuroplastic consequences (i.e., produces the most structural and/or functional brain changes) specifically because humans, to quote Atul Gawande, are "social creatures...simply to exist as a normal human being requires interaction with other people."

Consequently, the most prevalent and potent stressor among modern humans is rooted in our anxiety regarding how others perceive (or value) us. As social beings, explained Richard Wilkinson, "we monitor how others respond to us, so much so that it is sometimes as if we experienced ourselves through each other's eyes."

Threats to our social self, as stated by Tara Gruenewald et al., feature "situations that contain the potential to devalue one's social self by calling into question abilities, competencies, or traits on which a positive social image is based, or situations characterized by potential or explicit rejection. We assert that such situations are provocative because they contain social information pertinent to a

150

primary human goal: that of achieving and maintaining a positive 'social self.'"

"Humans are argued to be social animals that possess fundamental motivations to belong and be accepted by others, and the status of one's social self is argued to be an important determinant of the distribution of social and physical resources. Thus, concerns with achieving or maintaining a positive social self may be an important human motive that is supported by specific psychological and physiological systems that provide signaling (i.e., 'the social self is under threat') and mobilizing (i.e., initiation of psychobiological activity to help deal with the threat) functions."

Chronic devaluations of our social self—as a consequence of racial stigma experienced as racial trauma—prompt constant cortisol production and lasting maladaptive changes in certain brain areas, particularly the amygdala, hippocampus, and prefrontal cortex. Constant cortisol saturation significantly changes neural structures like the hippocampus and PFC, both of which are gradually reduced in size and activity as cortisol annihilates hippocampus and PFC neurons via prolonged overactivation. Conversely, continuous cortisol production increases the size and activity of the amygdala.

According to research by Pittenger and Duman, chronic race-based traumatic stress "enhances synaptic plasticity and the function of amygdala neurons, an effect quite distinct from the atrophy it induces in the hippocampus and PFC. This could both result from and contribute to overactivation of neuronal circuits that control fear, anxiety, and emotion," which could account for Black students' unique tendency to struggle with emotional self-regulation, impulsivity, and self-handicapping behavior in the classroom.

More Yesterday Than Anybody[29]
Acknowledging Intergenerational Poverty in America Tangibly and Stigmatically as Complex Trauma and Teaching Accordingly

"Higher income inequality intensities a community's hierarchy and makes social support less available: truly symmetrical, reciprocal, affiliative support exists only among equals. Moreover, having your nose rubbed in your poverty is likely to lessen your sense of control in life, to aggravate the frustrations of poverty and to intensify the sense of life worsening…the surest way to feel poor is to be made to feel poor—to be endlessly made aware of the haves when you are a have-not."
-Robert Sapolsky

"The poor in fact share the same values as the rest of society, but their behavior is a response to their perception of hopelessness in realizing these ideals."
-Peter Fekete

Intergenerational poverty, much like racism, "should be understood as an experience that can produce stress that in some cases can rise to the level of a traumatic stress reaction," explained Robert Carter et al. Students experiencing intergenerational

---

[29] Excerpted from the following Toni Morrison quote from *Beloved*: "Me and you, we got more yesterday than anybody. We need some kind of tomorrow."

poverty[30] live *lives* that are likely to be disproportionately ambiguous, negative, unpredictable, and uncontrollable (i.e., the four characteristic requirements for an experience to be considered traumatic). The omnipresent threat of poverty-related scarcity and susceptibility creates conditions ripe for chronic, braining-changing traumatic stress.

It is typically experienced (beginning in childhood) as "repeated instances of the same type of trauma over a period of time," which specifically qualifies as intergenerational poverty as complex trauma. It also "significantly increases the probability of a child being exposed to a set of other stressors that can become traumatic," noted Carlos Pitillas, which makes poverty usually experienced in addition to multiple trauma (e.g., emotional, sexual, or physical abuse; witnessing domestic violence; parental neglect or abandonment; homelessness or residential instability).

When students experience intergenerational poverty, they grow up with the omnipresent psychological and tangible threat of scarcity and inequity. They grow up somehow realizing that relative to everyone else, explained Charles Sackrey, "poor people are typically able to enjoy fewer goods, do fewer things, and achieve fewer goals than all those above them in higher-income classes." This realization itself can become chronically traumatic.

Poverty, according to Manning Marable, "must be understood properly as a comparative relationship between those segments of society who are deprived of basic human needs (e.g., food, shelter, clothing, medical care) vs. the most secure and affluent classes within a social and economic order."

To quote Melissa Phillips, poverty, particularly when intergenerational, is "a chronic fear of never having enough" to eat, to wear, to pay the rent or bills with. This chronic fear may certainly become traumatic once coupled with the terrible implication that we apparently may not possess the competence or

---

[30] As opposed to *situational poverty*, which does not persist into the next generation, is generally associated with a specific circumstance rather than systemic causes, and is somehow temporary.

resources necessary to ever stop being poor (i.e., develop the poverty mindset).

The "trauma that's associated with never having enough," observed Jessica Trudeau, becomes a "perpetual trauma." For students experiencing intergenerational poverty, "every day, they're on high alert, so their brain is literally being trained to respond in that matter." Intergenerational poverty can be an overwhelmingly stressful experience that forever changes a child's natural belief that the world is just and safe and *their* world is controllable.

"Chronic poverty changes the brain dramatically." These students, explained Eric Jensen, are "faced daily with overwhelming challenges that affluent children never have to confront, and their brains have adapted to suboptimal conditions" and "to reflect the environments they're in, not automatically rise above them." Consequently, they are inclined to "think of themselves as unworthy or unable to compete in labor markets, and that ultimately there is established a vicious circle of behavior in which the belief in one's inability to compete in labor markets leads to a lifestyle inconsistent with competition," including commitment to success in school.

Students "who have had greater exposure to poverty-related experiences are more reactive to stressors. Each stressor builds on and exacerbates other stressors and slowly changes the brain." The chronic stress of persistent poverty triggers continuous cortisol production which maladaptively increases the size and activity of the amygdala (while decreasing the size and activity of the hippocampus and prefrontal cortex). Students experiencing poverty as complex trauma will then be susceptible to heightened emotional reactivity due to a larger, hyperactive amygdala, especially since those brain structures (i.e., hippocampus and prefrontal cortex) that otherwise regulate negative emotion, memory, information processing, and impulsivity have been significantly diminished. Consequently, negative emotional reactions (e.g., anxiety, anger, impulsivity, frustration,

155

hopelessness, helplessness) are easier to generate and harder to regulate properly, leading to disruptive or self-handicapping classroom "behaviors that will likely puzzle, frustrate, or irritate teachers."

Oftentimes "school is not a priority for many students living in poverty," observed Regenia Rawlinson. "Often the circumstances of their lives leave them with serious stress. They confront hardship continuously. Some work a full-time job to help the family. Others may be their siblings' main caretakers. Some have the responsibility of caring for an alcoholic or addicted parent. Many live in substandard housing in crime-ridden neighborhoods and rarely have access to health care. Some walk the streets and stay out until late because they are unsupervised. Many live with a single parent and lack a male role model at home. A high percentage of children from single parent homes do not know their fathers. Some children juggle many such issues simultaneously. When they come to school, they are more tired than most other children. They are physically and emotionally drained."

These students oftentimes quickly lose hope that things will ever get better. "Many students in poverty have spotty-to-poor academic records that can often be linked to the poverty mindset that strips students of ambition and enthusiasm and makes them indifferent. Students with a poverty mindset often feel powerless and think they have no control over what happens in their lives. They blame their circumstances and other people and look to others to work things out for them. They attribute failure to their lack of ability" rather than their self-handicapping behaviors.

"Poverty shapes the mind for self-sabotage and possibly for self-destruction. Poverty makes people think they are unworthy. People who grow up in poverty accept and record the message of unworthiness and play the recording wherever they go. The tape plays, the act out the message. Counterproductive behaviors in the classroom may be evidence of the message."

"Educators do not accurately consider that the student is inundated with realities of poverty, like hunger pangs and neighborhoods littered with families in the same conditions—some only slightly more optimistic than others," detailed Diallotelli Brown. "Education does not seem to be a viable weapon to battle problems. Instead, education resembles a series of complex requirements that will not help the immediate situation. These conditions are the norm for many urban students who are not entirely engaged in learning. These students are conscious of how they live and subconsciously may see this as their adult life, too, even if they push hard to succeed in school."

Intergenerational poverty offers very little argument for being academically resilient. "If I'm just going to remain poor, why bother to try (so hard)? If I'm never going to not be poor, why not just quit now?" The insidious rationale of many students from high-poverty backgrounds ultimately becomes "since I didn't really try my best, then remaining poor is somehow not my fault (i.e., a reflection of personal/collective inadequacy). I won't feel even worse for having tried and failed like those before me. Better not to try." Quitting (or minimum effort) becomes a habit, which further underdevelops their academic resilience, disabling them from achieving academic success despite intergenerational poverty.

As students experiencing intergenerational poverty as complex trauma consistently withdraw from taking academic risks, relying on student-teacher relationships, and other pro-academic behaviors, the neural "circuitry for those activities begins to weaken," noted Norman Doidge. This atrophy is the consequence of neuronal connections not being reinforced via repetition as well as neuroplasticity attributable to experiencing chronic traumatic stress (and continuous cortisol saturation of certain brain areas) in connection with poverty as complex trauma.

They might try sporadically to be "good students," but "their brains will have trouble" with executing those unpracticed pro-academic behaviors, explained Eric Newhouse. Many of these students ultimately "develop something called learned non-use. Learned non-use is not a form of laziness; it is what the brain takes

157

away from repeated efforts to do something, and finding it can't...it will ultimately quit trying" and deploy "its resources in other areas."

Their brains tend to *maladapt* (i.e., change negatively) in order to simply survive their circumstances, most of which are uncontrollable and traumatic. Students experiencing intergenerational poverty are uniquely vulnerable to trauma-based maladaptive neuroplasticity and, consequently, tend to struggle with regulating negative emotions and impulsivity as well as overcoming their overreliance on self-handicapping academic behaviors.

Vanessa Jackson refers to intergenerational poverty as a potential "fiscal trauma," which she defined as an "intense emotional reaction, characterized by depression, anxiety/worry, a profound sense of shame, and a fear for survival in response to inadequate financial resources." The "life-threatening and shame-inducing experiences that result from inadequate income" could overwhelm an "individual's capacity to regulate their emotions" and "ability to cope with what they have experienced" and, consequently, become traumatic.

After decades of an inherited wealth gap, residential segregation, educational inequality, systemic labor obsolescence (via corporate suburbanization, automation, and globalization), calculated welfare dependency[31], affirmative inaction, an

---

[31]   Including the strategic increase in African-American welfare dependency as a strategy to thwart the urban uprisings of the late 1960s that literally ignited parts of every American city in hopes of sparking "Black Power."   White America was terrified, to quote J. Fred MacDonald, of the "the legitimate anger and frustration of African Americans trapped in the inner city by prejudice, poverty, ignorance, police power, and fear. Faced with unemployment, dilapidated ghettos, unfamiliar and subtle forms of discrimination, and handicapped by inadequate technical skills, by the mid-1960s many migrants abandoned established leadership and drifted into violence. Looting and burning often replaced passive resistance and religious principle. In 1967 alone,

there were eight major disorders, thirty-three serious outbreaks, and 133 minor disorders."

To many Americans "revolution seemed at hand following the assassination of Martin Luther King, Jr. in April 1968. Anger spilled into the streets, and armed troops were needed in many localities to reestablish social order. The image of U.S. Army soldiers bearing rifles in front of the Capitol, while streams of smoke rose in the background from the ghetto of Washington, D.C., told most dramatically the depth of this racial rage. Such pictures also revealed how disenchanted urban blacks had become with the passive resistance tactics of the early civil rights movement."

In response, the federal government initiated various policies, detailed James Button, "to prevent riots through welfare payments, low income housing, jobs programs—especially summer jobs programs for youths, which were seen as 'riot insurance.'" Christina Maimone cited that "cities that experienced a major riot had a significant increase in welfare spending and the number of individuals receiving welfare in the year after the riot."

Following the riots, the federal government continued to pacify Black people with welfare benefits (or remove with mass incarceration) as our socioeconomic obsolescence was drastically accelerated (due to rapid urban deindustrialization), yet the media's reaction was to cleverly advance the "all Blacks are lazy" stereotype. Martin Gilens recognized how "pictures of poor blacks were abundant when poverty coverage was most negative, while pictures of non-blacks dominated the more sympathetic media coverage." The media of the era was largely responsible for "the centuries old stereotype of blacks as lazy [remaining] credible for a large number of white Americans," who also erroneously believed that more Black people received welfare benefits than White.

Douglas Massey and Nancy Denton accurately identified that "as poverty rates rose among blacks in response to the economic dislocations of the 1970s and 1980s, so did the use of welfare programs. Because of racial segregation, however, the higher levels of welfare receipt were confined to a small number of isolated, all-black neighborhoods. By promoting the spatial concentration of welfare use, therefore, segregation created a residential environment within which welfare dependency was

159

entrepreneurship gap, and endemic joblessness, more and more students in America are experiencing intergenerational poverty. Income inequality continues to worsen as the poor are getting poorer and more permanently poor.

America is *supposed to be* the "land of opportunity," which essentially means that hard work and perseverance should result in intergenerational income mobility (i.e., children will grow up, make significantly more money, and, consequently, escape the confines of poverty experienced by their parents). In other words, America is generally perceived as the exemplar of a "society in which a child's chances of success depend little on his family background," noted Raj Chetty et al.

However, various structural barriers to intergenerational income (or social) mobility create such a consistent inequality of opportunity that the "chances of making it from a childhood in poverty to an adulthood in affluence are lower in the U.S. than in

---

the norm, leading to the intergenerational transmission and broader perpetuation of urban poverty."

Instigating welfare dependency concurrently promoted intergenerational poverty. Wilson confirmed that "food stamps, Medicaid, and the Supplemental Security Income program (SSI) do provide some relief, but as currently designed, they have virtually no effect on the continuing poverty rates among the nonelderly. In short, targeted programs for the poor in the United States do not even begin to address inequities in the social class system. Instead of helping to integrate the recipients into the broader economic and social life of mainstream society—to 'capitalize' them into a different educational or residential stratum, as the GI bill and the postwar federal mortgage programs did for working- and middle-class whites—they tend to stigmatize and separate them. As unemployment in the general population rises, the probability of exiting welfare diminishes. It is not surprising that those who are least employable in terms of skills and training are least successful in avoiding welfare."

As Sackrey realized, "the welfare system promises a little help for everyone, but not a lot for anyone, and, therefore, those currently on the bottom will continue to be there for some time."

160

other developed nations." In America, inequality, not mobility, is decidedly inherited. Rather than being the "land of opportunity," reported Richard Wilkinson, the "United States has unusually low rates of income mobility which seem to match its unusually large income difference."

A nation promotes social mobility "if it allows people to escape poverty while limiting the degree to which those who grow up in privileged homes get advantages throughout their lives," explained Emily Beller and Michael Hout. In America, established policies prefer to concentrate economic growth among the already wealthy, so there is very little "difference between a person's current income, wealth, or occupation and that of the family that raised" him or her. These policies have also increased inequality dramatically (i.e., income gap), particularly over the last 30 years. "An increase in inequality over a person's lifetime increases the probability that someone who starts life in extreme privilege will stay there and (simultaneously) increases the probability that someone whose parents were poor will also be poor."

More so in America than any other developed nation in the world, the incomes of parents can basically predict the incomes their children will have in adulthood; the children of poor parents typically remain poor as adults. This lack of intergenerational mobility begets the perpetuation and intensification of intergenerational poverty along with the potentially traumatic consequences of this poverty manifesting in young brains and classrooms across the country.

Going to and graduating from college right after high school is supposed to be a catalyst for intergenerational social mobility; however, a child's college ambition and participation is strongly proportional to their parent's income. Of course, there are exceptions (we're both such exceptions), but statistically it is far more likely that students of poor parents will neither genuinely aspire to[32] nor graduate from college, particularly not directly after

---

[32] Diminished college ambition has a direct effect on students' lack of academic resilience, self-efficacy, and other pro-academic behaviors in

high school. Instead of being the supposed "great social equalizer," a college education is effectively the great social immobilizer.

Where you live and who you are also impacts your chances of income mobility in America. For instance, living in cities in the South or Midwest hurts your chances drastically. Additionally, "upward income mobility is significantly lower in areas with larger African-American populations," observed Chetty et al. Even "white individuals in areas with large African-American populations have lower rates of upward mobility." Black children born to poor parents are far less likely to escape intergenerational poverty than other racial/ethnic groups, especially White Americans (and Black boys are more vulnerable than Black girls). "Black Americans have substantially lower rates of upward mobility and higher rates of downward mobility than whites, leading to large income disparities that persist across generations."

Educational inequality and endemic joblessness produce intergenerational poverty by sustaining (currently) poor people's (and their children's) vulnerability to remaining poor. Being poorly educated and ill-prepared for most of today's higher-paying, in-demand careers leaves people scrambling for limited, constantly low-paying, and oftentimes soon-to-be obsolete employment opportunities. This is true for all poor Americans, but it is especially true for poor Black people in America, whose opportunities for experiencing upward income mobility are further negated by residential segregation and racism.

Nationwide deindustrialization—the ultimate consequence of systemic labor obsolescence created by structural economic changes including corporate automation, suburbanization, and globalization—caused an unprecedented increase in joblessness (i.e., the permanent disappearance of blue-collar jobs) starting

---

grades 6-12 specifically. Consequently, students not motivated to work hard enough and find a way to be competitive in the college admission process will typically develop an overreliance on self-handicapping academic behaviors.

162

roughly in the late 1960s initially targeting (you guessed it) areas with larger African-American populations.

Over the following decades, an income and "employment gap between skilled and unskilled workers" explained William J. Wilson, "is growing partly because education and training are considered more than ever in the new global economy. At the same time that changes in technology are producing new jobs, they are making many others obsolete. While educated workers are benefiting from the pace of technological change involving the increased use of computer-based technologies and microcomputers, less skilled workers, such as those found in many inner-city neighborhoods, face the growing threat of job displacement."

"The steady advance of automation has raised the skill-level required to obtain steady employment," confirmed Louis Knowles. However, "no American institution has taken sufficient steps to ensure" that poor Americans "gain the skills necessary for entry into the modern job market."

Poor people have "traditionally held the jobs which are now being eliminated," noted Robert Allen. And the "pace of mechanization and automation, uneven though it is, cannot be halted because of the competitive need of individual corporations to increase efficiency and reduce costs in order to maintain profits and growth, and improve their relative standing vis-à-vis other companies. On the contrary, it can be expected that the pace of automation will accelerate, putting more minority groups and other workers without special skills out of work."

"The most-common occupations in the United States are retail salesperson, cashier, food and beverage server, and office clerk. Each is highly susceptible to automation," explained Derek Thompson. "Technology creates some jobs too, but the creative half of creative destruction is easily overstated. Nine out of 10 workers today are in occupations that existed 100 years ago, and just 5 percent of the jobs generated between 1993 and 2013 came from 'high tech' sectors like computing, software, and

163

telecommunications. Our newest industries tend to be the most labor-efficient: they just don't require many people."

"In the United States alone," concluded Jeremy Rifkin, "in the years ahead more than 90 million jobs in a labor force of 124 million are potentially vulnerable to replacement by automated machinery, robots, and increasingly sophisticated computers." Joblessness on a level heretofore unseen "seems all but inevitable in the coming decades," which ultimately means that exponentially more students in America will experience intergenerational poverty (potentially as complex trauma) as more work disappears, income inequality continues to worsen, and the poor get poorer and more permanently poor.

"Fewer jobs that pay living wages are being introduced into the American labor market," realized James Chambers. This is largely attributable to the "wealth of the nation continuing to be concentrated in the hands of a few; and to maximize profits, the wealthy are shipping jobs and industrial capabilities out of this country."

Bakari Kitwana confirmed that corporate "globalization has affected employment options for low-skilled workers in America by transnational corporations closing U.S. factories, laying off workers, and 'exporting' U.S. jobs to lower-wage workers abroad. While it's true that globalization has negatively affected all low-skilled, working-class Americans, older workers have fared better than younger ones, and Whites have fared better than Blacks."

Despite its structural causes, being poor in America is heavily stigmatized. Wilson described how poor Americans are generally seen as "a substantial minority of the population who share a common culture characterized by a lack of motivation to gain employment and who willingly depend upon the state for subsistence. Portraying people in this manner suggests that they are personally responsible for their own unemployment, poverty, and exclusion, rather than the unfortunate victims of structural economic change" and what John Galbraith termed the *equilibrium of poverty*.

164

The tangible realities of endemic joblessness, intergenerational poverty, and negated income mobility conspire to create this distinct psychological vulnerability that "destroys initiative, destroys energy, destroys the search for something better and, therefore, becomes self-perpetuating."

The intergenerationally poor having "lived at or near the minimum necessary for survival for a long time and here the condition persists because they live in an equilibrium of poverty. Few things allow for escape from life at a minimum level of subsistence; when something does, there are forces which operate to return the people to something approaching their former level of deprivation. Improving income here is not normal. It is and always has been unknown."

"We have observed the forces making for an equilibrium of poverty—that make poverty self-perpetuating and restore the previous level of deprivation, or something approaching it, if there is temporary improvement. But nothing so reinforces this equilibrium as the absence of aspiration—the absence of effort to escape it. In the poor community such aspiration, in turn, is in conflict with one of the most profound and predictable elements of human behavior. That is the refusal to struggle against the impossible, the tendency to prefer acquiescence to frustration."

"People do not strive, generation after generation, against circumstances that are so constituted as to defeat them. They accept. Nor is such acceptance a sign of weakness or character. Rather, it is a profoundly rational response. Given the formidable hold of the equilibrium of poverty within which they live, accommodation is the optimal solution. Poverty is cruel. A continuing struggle to escape that is continuously frustrated is more cruel. It is more intelligent, as well as more plausible, that people should reconcile themselves to what has for so long been the inevitable."

Natalia Fregoso agreed that "the poor in fact share the same values as the rest of society, but their behavior is a response to their perception of hopelessness in realizing these ideals. Poverty

165

creates a mindset, and certain beliefs about self and the world that limits perceptions, choices, motivations, and behaviors in ways that tend to perpetuate the condition."

Moreover, the idea that poor people "share more or less monolithic and predictable beliefs, values, and behaviors," noted Paul Gorski, is problematic yet it's also essential to the "culture of poverty" allegation. "There is no such thing as a culture of poverty. Differences in values and behaviors among poor people are just as great as those between poor and wealthy people. In actuality, the culture of poverty concept is constructed from a collection of smaller stereotypes which, however false, seem to have crept into mainstream thinking as unquestioned fact." Functionally, the true value of the culture of poverty argument is how efficiently it sanctions the stigma of intergenerational poverty.

Poverty in America can be a stigmatizing experience because, to quote Erving Goffman, it results in the possession of another socially defined "undesired differentness. Stigmatized persons possess an attribute," in this case *being poor*, "that is deeply discrediting and they are viewed as less than fully human because of it."

Poverty (i.e., being poor) as stigma is an "enduring condition, status, or attribute," according to Gregory Herek, "that is negatively valued by society, that fundamentally defines a person's social identity, and that consequently disadvantages and disempowers those who have it." However, "stigma is not inherent in a particular trait or membership in a particular group; rather, society collectively identifies particular characteristics or groups, and assigns negative meaning and value to some of them, thereby 'constructing' stigma."

In other words, being poor is not naturally defining, devaluing, or discrediting. Poverty didn't become a "negatively evaluated difference" until privilege and wealth needed to be justified. Being poor has become negatively perceived because we have been socialized to associate poverty with personal inadequacy or lack of effort as opposed to a consequence of structural inequality and

166

targeted joblessness. A negative meaning has been assigned to being poor in America, which somehow justifies structural inequality and targeted joblessness.

Antonio Rosales described how "research revealed that those who explained poverty through individualistic attributions had more negative attitudes towards the poor than those who explained it through structural attributions. Individualistic explanations of poverty emphasize that people are poor because of limitations related to the individual, while structural explanations refers to external forces such as society negatively acting upon the people." These negative attitudes generally evolve into negative meaning and value socially assigned to the intergenerationally poor, effectively "constructing" stigma. The norms, images, and messages within American culture have consistently affirmed the flawed belief that "economic outcomes are determined by an individual's efforts and talents (or their lack)," as explained by Wilson.

Residential segregation and social distance advance this stigmatizing delusion. Mike Rose argued that "if society separates groups of people physically and psychologically, it is easier for them to attribute inaccurate beliefs, thoughts, and motives to each other. These attributions have an effect on how people respond to poverty" and why "poor people are often associated with laziness" or lack of will (i.e., poor people choose to remain poor by not acting in ways that would end their poverty).

Even in their own classrooms, observed Rawlinson, "students living in poverty are often tagged as troublesome, dishonest, dumb, and lazy. They have to prove their innocence and ability before they get access to some educational opportunities. The opposite is true for more affluent students, who teachers presume are innocent and able. They get access to most places and educational opportunities without having to prove anything."

Poverty as stigma allows us to believe that it is not capitalism's inherent inequity that is at fault (i.e., causing poverty), it's the indolence, incompetence, or indifference (or culturally

167

inadequacy) of the poor. Poverty as stigma allows us to shift blame as an entire society and thwart social rebellion by creating, to cite Joe Pettit, "a hierarchical separation of human worth."

It's easier to see poverty stigmatically when the poverty is intergenerational. Intergenerational poverty can become perceptually associated with a specific group affiliation, since it (i.e., being poor) is a distinguishable, negative trait that can appear to be passed on from one generation to another in a particular social group (e.g., African-Americans). Because it *endures*, intergenerational poverty becomes perceived as an "enduring condition," which is a core requirement of stigma (as well as complex trauma).

As a result of stigma, there exists a "prevalence of erroneous negative beliefs about people in poverty," noted Declan Gaffney. Stigma, explained Megan Steinhardt, "allows one to make negative judgments based on the label a person is given rather than on any actual behavior." As a result of the stigma of poverty, poor people (students included) are generally seen as and expected to be lazy, trifling, incompetent, repugnant, and even dangerous. Behaviors that confirm this expectation are acknowledged (and typically even exaggerated) and those that don't are discounted as exceptional.

"When our American values of 'work harder and you will succeed' fail, we are quick to blame the individual rather than the system through which they are unable, not incapable, of succeeding in. The stigma then is perpetuated through society's misunderstanding of the individual's ability to get himself out of his situation." Their poverty, especially when intergenerational, is perceived as somehow their fault, a consequence of their own inherent inadequacy rather than structural inequality and endemic joblessness in contemporary America.

"The idea that individuals can escape poverty through hard work is a fundamental tenant of American society," explained Marianne Page et al., but "intergenerational mobility is lower in the United States than in any other developed country in the world." Nevertheless, the mere persistence of intergenerational

168

poverty becomes false confirmation of the appropriateness of the stigma attached to it.

Despite the true, structural causes of intergenerational poverty in America (e.g., corporate automation, globalization, residential segregation, educational inequality, welfare dependency), it inevitably begins to *appear* that specific social groups simply cannot stop being poor because of their own inherent inadequacy (as evidenced by its apparent inheritability). If these people *could* stop poverty they would have (since being poor sucks), so they must *cannot* (presumably because they are lazy, trifling, incompetent, repugnant, and probably dangerous). This fallacious but popular argument tends to prompt the stigma of poverty becoming complex trauma among the intergenerationally poor (especially when poverty as stigma is combined with another enduring stigma or trauma), who consequently develop a deeply ingrained feeling of shame, defectiveness, hopelessness, and helplessness (or uncontrollability).

Unfortunately, there is no minimum age requirement for this to occur, and students begin at an early age to continuously trigger traumatic stress responses as they tangibly and stigmatically experience intergenerational poverty. This experience oftentimes evolves into complex trauma as it overwhelms their "capacity to regulate their emotions" and "ability to cope with" what they are experiencing. Along with devaluing their self-concept and generating maladaptive neuroplasticity, intergenerational poverty as complex trauma can grossly underdevelop these students' self-efficacy in general and academic self-efficacy in particular.

Self-efficacy is an individual's (although there is a such thing as collective self-efficacy) beliefs about his or her ability to be perform certain behaviors successfully. Christine Fallon described self-efficacy as what "enables an individual to engage in goal-directed, self-regulated behavior even in the face of significant challenges to achievement or development."

"Self-efficacy is hypothesized to influence the choice and direction of much human behavior," noted Dale Schunk. High

169

self-efficacy is directly associated with increased academic motivation, persistence, and resistance to negative thinking with regard to academically adverse circumstances[33]. John Thompson defines self-efficacy as "the belief in one's ability to reach a certain outcome. Self-efficacy influences how hard one works, how often one participates, how long one persists in the face of adversity, and how highly one achieves."

Self-efficacy, according to Diane Craft and Patricia Hogan, is "the conviction that one is or is not capable of successfully performing the behavior required to produce a certain outcome, which affects whether or not a person will attempt a certain behavior and determines the effort expended and persistence levels." Whenever academic self-efficacy is underdeveloped, self-handicapping classroom behaviors tend to become commonplace as students become less and less likely to take responsibility for their academic success currently and quality of life as adults (including capacity to escape intergenerational poverty). Once we don't genuinely believe in our ability to achieve academically (or in the impact academic achievement will have on our capacity to escape intergenerational poverty), it's harder to resist quitting or acting out/being disruptive or exerting only minimal effort.

Self-efficacy is not about our actual ability to achieve but how we perceive our own ability, which is largely based on how others perceive that ability. Poverty as stigma makes this perception for poor people highly negative. Consistently negative reactions,

---

[33] To include lower teacher quality; a less impactful curriculum; lower per pupil expenditures; lower (i.e., stigma-influenced) teacher expectations regarding their academic performance; less effective classroom management; an overreliance on exclusionary discipline; higher student-to-teacher ratios; less access to new books, computers, the Internet, and other resources that stimulate or improve student engagement; a school climate generally less conducive to learning; practically nonexistent (or negligible at best) parental engagement and trust in the academic process; and significant (yet otherwise preventable) knowledge gaps.

perceptions, or expectations of others (e.g., parents, teachers, peers, society) and life experiences can diminish or not fully develop a child's level of self-efficacy as they grow into adulthood. All children don't equally learn how to persevere when they don't initially succeed and begin to anticipate failure.

"Chronic poverty changes the brain dramatically." Unfortunately for children experiencing intergenerational poverty, stigma coupled with "socioeconomic deprivation can create environments that undermine the development of self and the capacity for self-efficacy," concluded Jensen. The human brain is "designed to reflect the environment" it's in, "not to 'automatically' rise above it." Accordingly, with regard to students experiencing poverty or the stigma of poverty as complex trauma, they're "different" but only "because their brains are different" as a result of trauma-based maladaptive neuroplasticity.

Students experiencing intergenerational poverty "are more likely to give up or become passive and uninterested in school. This giving-up process is known as *learned helplessness.* It's not genetic; it's an adaptive"—or neuroplastic—"response to life conditions. And sadly, it frequently takes hold as early as 1st grade."

The chronic traumatic stress of persistent or intergenerational poverty (and poverty as stigma), much like the chronic traumatic stress of racism and racial stigma, triggers continuous cortisol production which maladaptively increases the size and activity of the amygdala (while decreasing the size and activity of the hippocampus and prefrontal cortex). Consequently, negative emotional reactions (e.g., anxiety, anger, frustration, shame, hopelessness, helplessness) are easier to generate and harder to regulate.

"Chronic stress increases the complexity of neurons in the amygdala, the brain's emotion center" and "often results in a condition known as allostatic load. Allostatic load is 'carryover' stress. Instead of returning to a healthy baseline of homeostasis, the brain adapts to negative life experiences so that it becomes

171

either hyper-responsive or hypo-responsive." With regard to emotional reactivity, hyper-responsive generates antagonism and aggression and hypo-responsive produces indifference and apathy. People "who have had greater exposure to poverty-related experiences are more reactive to stressors. Each stressor builds on and exacerbates other stressors and slowly changes the brain."

Carol Miller and Cheryl Kaiser confirmed that not only can poverty as "stigma be a source of chronic stress for stigmatized people," it can ultimately become a complex traumatic stressor specifically because stigma is highly uncontrollable and experienced as a "repeated instance of the same type of trauma over a period of time" or in addition to other types of traumatic stressors. Complex trauma involves recurring, prolonged, or cumulative exposure to trauma-inducing situations; stigma can certainly be such a situation.

Threats to our social self, observed Tara Gruenewald et al., feature "situations that contain the potential to devalue one's social self by calling into question abilities, competencies, or traits on which a positive social image is based, or situations characterized by potential or explicit rejection. We assert that such situations are provocative because they contain social information pertinent to a primary human goal: that of achieving and maintaining a positive 'social self.'" Intergenerational poverty is such a situation.

Not unlike racial stigma, the stigma of intergenerational poverty is a *social evaluative threat*, which means it attacks our self-concept or social value (i.e., our social self). According to new neuroscientific evidence, social evaluative threats trigger the kind of traumatic stress that has the greatest neuroplastic consequences (i.e., produces the most structural and/or functional brain changes) specifically because humans, to quote Atul Gawande, are "social creatures...simply to exist as a normal human being requires interaction with other people."

Consequently, the most prevalent and potent traumatic stressor among modern humans is rooted in our anxiety regarding how others perceive (or value) us. As social beings, explained Richard

172

Wilkinson, "we monitor how others respond to us, so much so that it is sometimes as if we experienced ourselves through each other's eyes. Given that the social hierarchy is seen as a hierarchy from the most valued at the top, to the least valued at the bottom, it is easy to see how bigger status differences increase the evaluative threat and add to status competition and status insecurity."

Poverty as stigma is "more common where there is more inequality not only because inequality increases status competition, but also because people deprived of the markers of status (incomes, jobs, houses, cars, etc.) become particularly sensitive to how they are seen. What hurts about having second-rate possessions is being seen as a second-rate person. Increased social hierarchy and inequality substantially raises the stakes and anxieties about personal worth throughout society. We all want to feel valued and appreciated, but a society which makes large numbers of people feel they are looked down on, regarded as inferior, stupid and failures," can normalize experiencing poverty as complex trauma.

Phillips described intergenerational poverty as "a chronic fear of never having enough." Much of its traumatic stress is derived from this chronic fear (i.e., the threat of scarcity) and the terrible implication that we may not possess the competence or resources necessary to stop being poor. Poor people, particularly those experiencing persistent poverty, oftentimes develop a poverty consciousness (much like racially stigmatized people develop stigma consciousness). Jeanie Marshall defined poverty conscious as a "set of attitudes and beliefs and feelings and values associated with material lack or fear of material lack. Poverty consciousness equals a belief in limitation and almost always includes fear."

For students, intergenerational poverty must be understood "not only as a negative experience, an instance of social exclusion, injustice, an adverse experience or a corrosive disadvantage," explained Carlos Pitillas, "but as a potentially traumatic experience." Intergenerational poverty drastically increases the probability of a student being continuously exposed to multiple

173

potentially traumatic adverse childhood experiences, including microinequities[34]; food insecurity; inadequate or inconsistent housing; unreliable transportation; undesirable or socially rejected clothing options; displaced parental frustration; lack of access to quality health care; disproportionate exposure to community crime and violence; environmental injustice; criminal injustice and frequent familial incarceration; and other daily hassles associated with inadequate access to resources and opportunities.

And whenever "fiscal trauma intersects with racial oppression," noted Lillian Drakeford, the traumatic stress under which Black students experiencing intergenerational poverty live can ultimately produce an innate rage or indifference ready to explode whenever exposed to any additional classroom stressor, such as criticism, confrontation, or perceived inadequacy. Hence, the urgent need for more *fully* trauma-informed educators in schools that are high-poverty and have higher percentages of African-American students.

"The severity and chronicity of reactions to repeated traumas traditionally focus on the cumulative effects of multiple traumatic episodes." Yet, circumstances such as race and intergenerational poverty that "create persistent feelings of not being safe and of being unable to control situations cause children to anticipate further events even as they deal with the effects of past trauma," explained Kathryn Collins et al. Consequently, "it is the combination of experience and anticipation of traumatic events" that leads to trauma-based maladaptive neuroplasticity.

---

[34] Mary Rowe defined microinequities, a specific type of microstressor, as "apparently small events which are often ephemeral and hard-to-prove, events which are covert, often unintentional, frequently unrecognized by the perpetrator, which occur wherever people are perceived to be 'different.'" They are seemingly innocuous yet persistent "messages of devaluation" that include casual discriminatory behaviors "such as being ignored, avoided, excluded, belittled, or treated with less courtesy and respect."

Holding Fast to a Doomed Fly's Wings[35]
Why Knowing Trauma Is Not an Excuse for "Bad" Students (and Not Knowing Trauma Doesn't Excuse "Bad" Teaching)

"We look at our youth and say that they're bad. I like to say they're hurting. Their behaviors are behaviors of them acting out pain. They're just trying to meet a need—the need to be included, to be loved, to be welcomed, respected, and wanted. Everybody wants to be wanted."

-Ayize Ma'at

"There's this whole population of kids we refer to as overcorrected, overdirected, and overpunished. Anyone who works with kids who are behaviorally challenging knows these kids: They've habituated to punishment. Behaviorally challenging kids are still poorly understood and are still being treated in ways that are adversarial, reactive, punitive, unilateral, ineffective, counterproductive. Not only are we not helping, we are going about doing things in ways that make things worse."

-Ross Greene

"I care. I care about it all. It takes too much energy not to care."

-Lorraine Hansberry

---

[35] Excerpted from the following Walter Mosley quote from *When the Thrill is Gone*: "Many and most moments go by with us hardly aware of their passage. But love and hate and fear cause time to snag you, to drag you down like a spider's web holding fast to a doomed fly's wings."

176

Students impacted by complex trauma *still want to learn* and be successful, even as they struggle with regulating negative emotions and impulsivity as well as overcoming their overreliance on self-handicapping academic behaviors. "Focusing on academics while struggling with trauma," to quote Ray Wolpow et al., "is like trying to play chess in a hurricane." Consequently, it seems illogical (if not foolish) to expect students experiencing complex trauma (at least, but usually in addition to, race-based experiences or intergenerational poverty) to succeed academically and behave appropriately, while we as teachers and administrators remain *willfully* ignorant of the evidence-based impact and interventions associated with trauma-based maladaptive neuroplasticity.

Or unwilling to teach these students about trauma, neuroplasticity, impulse control, resilience, and emotional regulation because we "can't find enough time" to do so while concurrently covering enough content to get test scores high enough to maintain our employment.

Or reluctant to use this information to better understand and respond to negative student behavior, especially the pervasive self-handicapping academic behavior of Black and poor students, as opposed to hastily labeling these students as innately incompetent (i.e., not capable of learning), disinterested in learning, unteachable, or generally incorrigible *because* they are Black and poor[36].

---

[36] The negative academic behavior of Black and poor students is typically (if not automatically) seen as confirmation of stigma-based expectations rather than a consequence of trauma-based maladaptive neuroplasticity. The stigma attached to Blackness and poverty in America creates a general expectation that Black and poor people possess certain negative characteristics simply because they are Black and/or poor, to include being unintelligent, inadequate, indifferent, lazy, disrespectful, unaccountable, troublesome, and uncontrollable. This expectation compromises our otherwise instinctive capacity to respond to these students with unconditional compassion and positive regard

It's particularly irrational to continue to do so in schools that are high-poverty and/or have higher percentages of African-American students because these schools also have higher percentages of *probably traumatized* students (i.e., students most likely experiencing complex trauma and trauma-based maladaptive neuroplasticity at least as a consequence of race or poverty) than their more affluent and/or White counterparts.

Considering the predictably traumatic impact of race and intergenerational poverty, instead of the 25-40% of potentially traumatized students in "normal" schools, in *these* schools we're possibly looking at closer to 80-90% of students presumably having already been exposed to (and their brains negatively changed by) complex trauma. These students, observed Eric Jensen, "are different because their brains are different. Our brains are designed by nature to reflect the environments they're in"— inclusive of negative race or poverty-based experiences these students may endure repeatedly and in addition to other trauma— "not to 'automatically' rise above them."

Accordingly, success in these school *requires* educators to have some type of intentional, systemic focus on strategically supporting and improving *all* students' capacity to regulate their negative emotions and impulsivity, sustain positive relationships, and reduce their overreliance on self-handicapping behaviors as opposed to simply responding to them more conditionally and negatively. This focus will concurrently strengthen all students' capacity to demonstrate higher levels of academic engagement, self-efficacy, self-resilience, and achievement as measured by state assessments.

If "every school in our country should have trauma-informed staff and consultants providing school-based trauma-specific treatment," why do so many teachers and administrators choose to

---

(perhaps out of fear of discovering stigma-contradicting circumstances or appearing to endorse excuses for the behavior), but responding to all students with unconditional compassion and positive regard is essential to truly being a trauma-informed educator.

178

remain willfully ignorant, unwilling, and reluctant as opposed to becoming trauma-informed?

"We can easily forgive a child who is afraid of the dark," to quote Plato, "the real tragedy of life is when men are afraid of the light."

It appears that trauma-ignorance remains the implicit norm throughout many American schools largely because American educators remain afraid of somehow being perceived as (more) indifferent, intimidated, and/or ineffective, especially with regard to Black and poor students.

Most of us initially and incorrectly associate being trauma-informed with lowering our academic and behavioral expectations of students apparently experiencing trauma. Knowing trauma (and trauma-based maladaptive neuroplasticity) is not an excuse for lower academic expectations or to not discipline negative student behavior. Being trauma-informed doesn't imply indifference or intimidation. Being trauma-informed does not somehow mean that teachers and school administrators can't hold *all* of their students accountable. Holding a potentially (if not probably) traumatized student accountable is just more restorative and strategic as opposed to simply punitive and instructionally straightforward.

For most educators, the worst accusation you can make against them is that they have lowered or negative academic and behavioral expectations for certain (e.g., Black or poor) students. Having lowered expectations, consciously or unconsciously, is terrible because "those for whom low expectations are held are taught in a manner that guarantees low levels of achievement," explained Thomas Brown. "Students for whom teachers hold low expectations for academic achievement are taught less effectively than those for whom high expectations are held. In general, students who are not expected to make significant progress experience limited opportunities to engage actively in the learning process."

Kenneth Clark noted that these students "are not being taught; and not being taught, they fail. They have a sense of personal

179

humiliation and unworthiness. They react negatively and hostilely and aggressively to the educational process. They hate teachers, they hate schools, they hate anything that seems to impose upon them this denigration, because they are not being respected as human beings, because they are sacrificed in a machinery of efficiency and expendability, because their dignity and potential as human beings are being obscured and ignored."

"The fact that these children, by and large, do not learn because they are not being taught effectively and they are not being taught because those who are charged with the responsibility of teaching them do not believe that they can learn, do not expect that they can learn, and do not act toward them in ways which help them to learn."

Teacher expectations, explained Nooe Chere and Dipane Hlalele, have a tendency to "be self-fulfilling. In self-fulfilling prophecy, the teacher's beliefs about students' abilities have no basis, but student behavior comes to match the initially inaccurate expectations. Though expectations may be inaccurate, they determine how teachers view and interact with the learners." These students are generally focused on negatively in school by educators and offered low reinforcement for positive academic behaviors and attitudes, prompting persistent, counterproductive responses from many of these students that otherwise may not have occurred.

Traumatized students' academic behavior is influenced by their teachers' negative expectations to a far greater extent than other students because their self-concept—how we think about, evaluate, and perceive ourselves—has already been impaired (i.e., negatively biased) as a result of experiencing complex trauma.

However, this is typically *not* why most teachers are afraid to reveal lowered expectations for certain students. We wish it was, but it's not. Unfortunately, it's a far more selfish reason than not wanting to teach "in a manner that guarantees low levels of achievement." That reason: teacher job security.

180

The mere perception that a teacher possesses lowered or negative expectations for certain students is enough to jeopardize their current and future employment opportunities. Why? *School administrator* job security.

The thing nearly all teachers (at least those with few other comparably paying career options) fear the most is a negative evaluation because negative evaluations can directly impact their job security. Contemporary teacher evaluations typically include a required minimum target of their students' growth (or raw score) on state-mandated testing. If their students do not reach this target growth (or score), the teacher is somehow penalized on their evaluation (e.g., labeled minimally effective or ineffective). Negative evaluations can ultimately get your teacher contract nonrenewed and send you looking for a new job (or career).

Teaching with lowered student expectations is typically considered to be one of the most obvious causes of low student scores on state-mandated testing. A teacher's effectiveness is now largely based on their students' state-mandated test scores. Low student test scores suggest teacher ineffectiveness. Proof or perception of lowered expectations creates explicit accountability on the part of the teacher. In other words, lowered expectations can create an unambiguous reason for the low student test scores or to at least blame the teacher for the scores.

Most teachers would not willingly jeopardize their employment by being accused of having lowered or negative student expectations for certain students, which is why they generally try so hard to *conceal* them. Most only pretend to believe that all children can learn at high levels (while having daily peer conversations about why they can't teach certain students who "don't want to learn"). However, "as with the formation of expectations based on inappropriate factors," observed Kathleen Cotton, the "communication of differential expectations is often unconscious on the part of teachers." As a teacher it is extremely difficult, if not impossible, to consistently conceal your expectations. Even when *you're* not conscious of your

181

expectations, your students may very well be (especially those students already hypervigilant from experiencing trauma).

Biased teacher expectations of certain students often create what Robert Tauber refers to as "expectation-revealing perceiver expressive behaviors"—behaviors that suggest to someone what we expect from them. These expressive behaviors may be verbal or nonverbal, unintentional or deliberate. Either way, our "expectations influence such expressive behaviors, and these behaviors influence the actions of others."

No school administrator wants to knowingly employ a teacher that seems to possess lowered or negative expectations for certain students because that teacher is more likely to teach in a way that guarantees low scores on state-mandated testing. Administrators are ultimately held accountable by Superintendents and School Boards for raising their students' scores on state-mandated testing (i.e., student achievement is also a significant part of administrator evaluation), so employing teachers with low expectations directly jeopardizes their own job security. And since a new administrative position is numerically harder to secure than a new teacher position, most administrators fear a negative evaluation more than their teachers do.

So, if being trauma-informed as a teacher or administrator is somehow perceived, even erroneously, as having lowered academic expectations of certain students, then it is *safer* to remain trauma-ignorant.

Or perhaps the real reason for our sustained reluctance with regard to being trauma-informed is something far more dubious. "Sometimes a man wants to be stupid," wrote John Steinbeck, "if it lets him do a thing his cleverness forbids." What if most educators simply have no desire to work harder to be trauma-informed? In other words, what if simple *laziness*, not perceived expectations, is the most tangible motive behind why so many educators remain willfully ignorant of the evidence-based impact and interventions associated with trauma-based maladaptive neuroplasticity.

182

It's already hard enough working with all of the academically adverse circumstances[37] common in schools that are high-poverty and/or have higher percentages of African-American students. Becoming and remaining a trauma-informed educator requires a unique level of effort. Regrettably, too many teachers and administrators prefer to exert minimum effort, only enough to maintain employment regardless of effectiveness.

Throughout American public education and its millions of educators there is collective norm of minimum effort, which is largely[38] why "too many American schools are still failing," explained Karl Weber. They are "failing to prepare students adequately for higher education and for the challenging workplaces of the future; they are failing to produce the large numbers of high-skilled professionals our country will need to remain economically competitive; and they are, most egregiously, failing to provide students from ethnic and racial minorities, as well as the

---

[37] To include lower teacher quality; a less impactful curriculum; lower per pupil expenditures; cumulative effect of historically lower (i.e., stigma-influenced) teacher expectations regarding their academic performance; less effective classroom management; an overreliance on exclusionary discipline; higher student-to-teacher ratios; less access to new books, computers, the Internet, and other resources that stimulate or improve student engagement; a school climate generally less conducive to learning; practically nonexistent (or negligible at best) parental engagement and trust in the academic process; and significant (yet otherwise preventable) knowledge gaps.

[38] But not *exclusively*. Not all American public schools are failing equally. Much of this failure disproportionately impacts minority and poor students. Danielle Lavin-Loucks realized that the "sheer presence of an achievement gap based on race, ethnicity, and socioeconomic status implies an unequal educational system. Predicated on race and class divisions, the achievement gap is part of a larger legacy that intertwines individual and family resources with school quality, social capital, and educational opportunity." It is the direct consequence of the "pervasive nature of school inequality, institutionalized racism, and segregation," not just the minimum effort of teachers and administrators.

economically disadvantaged, with the intellectual tools they need to achieve their piece of the American dream."

Being a trauma-informed educator is hard, additional work, especially in schools with high percentages of probably traumatized students. Realizing the impact of trauma; recognizing the signs and symptoms of trauma in our students; responding with evidence-based supports, interventions, and policies to those students; and also actively resisting retraumatization (i.e., triggering trauma)—all while teaching possibly hundreds of students daily—can be categorically hard work. And too many teachers and administrators would prefer to not work *that* hard (even if paid more).

Besides, in all honesty, most of us can get away with not being effective or trauma-informed—especially when we work in schools that are high-poverty and/or have higher percentages of African-American students—because many (if not most) Superintendents, School Boards, and the public at large are either more or less trauma-ignorant or generally reluctant to use trauma-informed strategies to better understand and respond to negative student performance. And their reluctance is mostly based on semiconsciously accepting negative performance of Black and poor students as confirmation of stigma-based expectations rather than the consequence of possible trauma-based maladaptive neuroplasticity.

Or maybe it's not willful ignorance or fear of job insecurity or laziness at all, but actually a *benign* (yet pervasive) ignorance among educators with regard to teaching with trauma in mind. Trauma-informed teaching is still a relatively new and unfamiliar concept. You can't do what you just don't know. And, according to Socrates, "you don't know what you don't know" (unless you're reading this book, in which case, you now know a lot and no longer have the defense of benign ignorance...#sorrynotsorry).

Trauma-informed teaching and administrating can't ever be just "one more thing" we ask teachers and administrators to do. And it shouldn't be, because being trauma-informed is intended to

184

support and enhance our effectiveness as teachers and administrators just as much as it ultimately supports our students' academic success.

Helping our students regulate their negative emotions, impulsivity, and overreliance on self-handicapping academic behavior by seeing them as potentially (if not probably) traumatized individuals unwittingly attempting to "survive in the moment," free of stigma and fully capable of learning at high levels, is vital to high-quality teaching and administrating (and, consequently, improving student scores of state-mandated testing). Perhaps just as vital is concurrently increasing our capacity to respond to these students strategically with evidence-based supports, interventions, and policies.

"Positive teaching conditions and a good school environment are unequally distributed over schools and are related to the demographic composition of the student population," concluded Jaap Dronkers. Schools with many disruptive, knowledge deficient[39], and probably traumatized "students have less opportunity to become and remain effective. The learning and teaching time at such schools is continually under pressure because time is lost on student problems that are not related to learning. The risk then arises that the teaching staff will eventually give up the fight for quality in their teaching." We've seen this logic play out repeatedly all around us, essentially sacrificing the already

---

[39] Michael Porter differentiates between students being "knowledge deficient" as opposed to innately deficient (i.e., deficient because they are Black or poor). "Children who are knowledge deficient do not have command of certain skills and concepts that have been mastered by the average child of the same age and with the same amount of time spent in schooling. More specifically, these children have not learned many of the things it is expected that they would have learned at any given point during their school experience."

185

compromised life chances[40] of thousands of Black and poor students. You've probably seen it too.

Being trauma-informed, particularly for those of us working in schools that are high-poverty and/or have higher percentages of African-American students, is akin to that famous passage from Sun Tzu's *The Art of War*, which "teaches us to rely not on the likelihood of the enemy's not coming, but on our own readiness to receive him; not on the chance of his not attacking, but rather on the fact that we have made our position unassailable."

Although any child could experience complex trauma, students already experiencing racial injustice, inequality, and stigma or intergenerational poverty are more likely to experience it (and possibly additional events or circumstances) as complex trauma and, consequently, are more vulnerable to trauma-based maladaptive neuroplasticity. Accordingly, we who teach them are definitely going to disproportionately experience students impacted by complex trauma and who, as a result, tend to struggle with regulating negative emotions and impulsivity as well as overcoming their overreliance on self-handicapping academic behaviors.

We are definitely going to disproportionately experience students who engage in disruptive classroom antics, apathy, absenteeism, noncompliance, incompetence, excuses, vulgarity, and misplaced aggression. Oftentimes, school gradually stops being understood as a priority for students experiencing childhood trauma. Survival, or rather, somehow dealing the fear of not surviving, semiconsciously becomes too much of a priority, leaving their trauma-changed brain little room to focus on sustaining pro-academic behavior.

"Our brains are wired to protect us from threat," noted Isaiah Pickens and Nicole Tschopp, "and no experience better represents threat than a traumatic event." A student's brain, once changed by complex trauma, tends to function in a constant state of fight or

---

[40] The opportunities each individual has to improve his or her quality of life.

flight, anticipate or perceive threat (especially psychological threat) where there is none, and struggle to manage negative emotions in order to shift from the survival-oriented brain to the learning-ready brain when required. In reaction to past trauma, their survival-oriented brain has been distinctly reformed and repurposed to now automatically and primarily *anticipate* future trauma (regardless of accuracy or evidence and inclusive of the potentially traumatic psychological threat of anticipated inadequacy and failure) as a defense mechanism.

Most educators expect their students to "come into an academic environment ready to both learn and emotionally experience the enjoyment and excitement of discovery." However, according to Basha Krasnoff, brain changes caused by complex trauma "often block a child's ability to learn in the classroom. Children and adolescents are overwhelmed by the way their brains react to prolonged stress or trauma" by becoming "endlessly vigilant. Traumatized youth will do anything to survive—not because they want to but because they need to."

They stop taking enough of the positive academic risks (e.g., giving maximum effort, effectually responding to teacher checks for understanding, adequately studying for assessments, taking advantage of academic supports as needed) required for learning. Their brain tends to uniquely process these risks as most likely becoming shame-inducing experiences based on the perceived psychological threat of anticipated inadequacy and failure. Such experiences, like their previous or ongoing trauma, are expected to somehow overwhelm their "capacity to regulate their emotions" and "ability to cope with what they have experienced" and, consequently, become traumatic (or trauma triggers).

As students experiencing complex trauma consistently withdraw from taking academic risks, relying on student-educator relationships, and other pro-academic behaviors, the neural "circuitry for those activities begins to weaken," noted Doidge. This atrophy is the consequence of neuronal connections not being reinforced via repetition as well as neuroplasticity attributable to

187

experiencing chronic traumatic stress (and continuous cortisol saturation of certain brain areas) in connection with their complex trauma. They might try sporadically to be "good students," but "their brains will have trouble" with executing those unpracticed pro-academic behaviors, explained Eric Newhouse.

We are definitely going to disproportionately experience moments in which all thought and behavior in that moment—even if disruptive or self-handicapping—is psychological (and sometimes even physical) survival-oriented. Our student's primary concern in that moment (as opposed to learning from or listening to you) is somehow stopping the negative emotions associated with the perceived threat without having adequate access to those parts of the human brain that typically stop negative emotions. The reply then becomes using other/more negative emotions (and emotional behavior) to try to stop the negative emotions currently being experienced, which is akin to attempting to extinguish a housefire by using other/more fire.

We shouldn't rely on the likelihood of these trauma-changed students not being or these trauma-based experiences not occurring in our classes and schools, but on our professional readiness to receive them strategically.

"Few events outside the classroom have as profound an impact on multiple domains of student development as traumatic life experiences," explained Pickens and Tschopp. Numerous studies have confirmed that complex trauma can terribly undermine a student's ability to behave appropriately and achieve their academic potential. Thus, educators must be familiar with and proficient in trauma-informed responses designed to mitigate trauma's impact in the classroom. They must also become skilled in facilitating practices, tools, and opportunities intended to increase their "students' abilities to manage interpersonal challenges related to traumatic experiences" consistently and independently, especially when these challenges become normative and easier to erroneously "attribute to immutable character traits" or stigma.

188

Ideally, all students who experience trauma would receive professional, consistent "therapy by qualified psychologists, psychiatrists, and/or social workers. However," noted Tom Brunzell et al., "many students and their families lack access, motivation, and ability to successfully participate in therapy. Although teachers are not therapists, and are neither trained nor prepared to delve into personal trauma histories with their students, they often find themselves acting as front-line trauma healers in the context of the classroom for young people who do not have access to clinical care."

But these teachers will need training, lots of ongoing training and modeling (and some incentivizing), in (for) using research and practice-based actionable strategies proven to support students impacted by complex trauma with regulating negative emotions and impulsivity as well as overcoming their overreliance on self-handicapping academic behaviors. In fact, not only will teachers need training, but *every adult in the building* needs to be trained on trauma-informed practices in order to become a trauma-informed school.

Without this training, instructional and support staff who continue to work in schools with a high percentage of students experiencing complex trauma will "continue to work in less than optimal situations with less than adequate research-proven skills, strategies, and understanding to address and remove the barriers that chronic traumatic stress creates in the lives of their students." Instead of practicing "thoughtful and intentional kindness," "authentic care for their students in structured, measurable ways," and "unconditional respect and empathy," they will continue to overreact to, hastily label, over-penalize, underteach, and unjustly exclude[41] students acting and emoting in negative ways "as a result of the trauma they have experienced."

---

[41]   According to Anita Wadhwa, an overreliance on exclusionary discipline (i.e., office referral, special education placement, suspension, and expulsion) "might be understandable if the policy were found to successfully curb or improve behaviors such as truancy, fighting, and

Wolpow et al. observed that they are also at a greater "risk of burnout" and vicarious trauma[42], which results "from the mirror neurons of the students passing on their traumatic stress to the mirror neurons of the teachers, administrators, and staff. Without knowledge, skills, and strategies to minimize this impact, educators' physical and mental health will be affected, increasing absenteeism, and contributing to their leaving the profession" or schools that are high-poverty and/or have higher percentages of African-American students.

Memorable or committed exposure to just one trauma-informed educator (and their strategic approach) can make a significant difference in a traumatized student's capacity to overcome their brains having maladapted to "suboptimal conditions in ways that undermine good school performance."

While there is no magic bullet for "fixing" trauma-affected students, there's extensive data revealing schools that persistently

---

verbal disrespect—behaviors that administrators have reported as the most prevalent and worrisome in their day-to-day school experiences. However, a substantial body of literature is pointing to the failure of exclusionary discipline to create safer schools or improve student behavior." Researchers have generally agreed that reactive, punitive, and exclusionary approaches have never been effective, and are the major reason why the number of students with problem behavior has significantly increased. Simply punishing students for their problem behaviors is directly associated with increases in those problem behaviors.

[42] Vicarious (or secondary) trauma, explained Wolpow et al., results from "internalizing the traumatizing event experienced by another" (e.g., traumatized students). "It is not uncommon for school professionals, who have a classroom with one or more students struggling with the effects of trauma, to experience symptoms very much like those their students are exhibiting. These symptoms are called vicarious or secondary trauma. (Vicarious: to feel through the experience of others; a secondary experience of the trauma rather than primary one.) It can affect...our ability to reason, our ability to be empathetic, and how we relate to others" (especially our traumatized students).

train and encourage staff to practice various trauma-informed responses benefit from improved scores on state-mandated testing, grade point averages, graduation rates, school culture and climate, teacher-administrator trust, and staff morale and retention. These trauma-informed schools also experienced significant reductions in disruptive student behavior, the overuse of administrative referrals, special education placements, student truancy, detentions, and suspensions.

Attempting to hold a potentially (if not probably) traumatized student accountable to high expectations, if the attempt is to be successful, must be more restorative and strategic as opposed to simply punitive and instructionally straightforward. It's worth noting that not every difficult or failing or self-handicapping student has experienced complex trauma, but too many of them have.

Yet, most educators have never been trained in identifying and reacting strategically to probably traumatized students. Educators are somehow expected to increase tests scores and manage classrooms (or oversee buildings) in which well over half of the students may be experiencing chronic traumatic stress, and we are penalized if we can't. "High-stakes testing—defining students by a test score—goes against everything research is telling us about how to help struggling with trauma," observed Jim Sporleder. "It also leads to hostile environments where extremely stressed teachers are working with highly stressed students." Consequently, many teachers still rely overwhelmingly on obsolete, hostile practices of threatening, yelling at, arguing with, labeling, failing, punishing, and excluding students, many of whom *are* experiencing complex trauma (at least, but usually in addition to, race-based experiences or intergenerational poverty).

"No curriculum, instruction, or assessment," noted Jensen, "however high quality will succeed in a hostile" classroom and school culture. However, teacher-student hostility becomes commonplace in trauma-ignorant classrooms and schools as both teachers and students maladapt (i.e., change negatively) in order to simply survive an emotional atmosphere that reeks of mutual overwhelmedness, fatigue, frustration, disappointment, joylessness, hopelessness, anxiety, anger, neglect, shame, disrespect, and helplessness.

Demonstrating *unconditional positive regard* for all students is arguably the most fundamental quality of the trauma-informed educator. Alex Shevrin described unconditional positive regard as "the belief that every student is worthy of care and that worth is not contingent on anything—not compliance with rules, not good behavior, not academic success." Consequently, when we practice unconditional positive regard, nothing our students do should ever motivate us "to stop seeing them as inherently human and lovable," confirmed Courtney Ackerman. This "does not mean that you accept each and every action taken by the person, but that you accept who they are at a level much deeper than surface behavior" and promote logical consequences for negative behavior. This is specifically relevant in educator relationships with students impacted by trauma.

Without it, all the research and practice-based actionable strategies in the world can only conceal and delay the consequences of its absence. Educators aspiring to be trauma-informed, particularly those working in schools that are high-poverty and/or have higher percentages of Black students, must be able to clearly and sometimes aggressively articulate just what makes them demonstrate unconditional positive regard to *these* students *irrespective of* the aforementioned emotional atmosphere.

"Survival and emotional data have priority over cognitive processing," acknowledged David Sousa, especially those students already hypervigilant from experiencing complex trauma. Students experiencing trauma-based neuroplasticity consequently have brains that are especially perceptive to and preoccupied with negative external stimuli. A student's brain, once changed by complex trauma, tends to function in a constant state of fight or flight, anticipate or perceive threat (especially psychological threat) where there is none, and struggle to manage negative

192

emotions in order to shift from the survival-oriented brain to the learning-ready brain when required. These brain changes, noted Jensen, can control not just their brains but "their feelings and their behaviors" as well, "and those three run their cognition" (including core academic activity such as learning, thinking, remembering, and problem solving).

In other words, students experiencing trauma-based neuroplasticity learn best when they can believe those teaching them genuinely care about them, which is most efficiently demonstrated via unconditional positive regard. Showing we "care has more of an effect on student motivation than our level of content knowledge," concluded Jensen. When we are compassionate, "enthusiastic, and engaged, our students will feel more excited about learning and will almost always work harder." Unlike their untraumatized counterparts who can succeed regardless, these students essentially *require* believable compassion from their educators in order to begin to reverse some of the maladaptive neuroplasticity preventing them from consistently practicing pro-academic behavior.

To paraphrase Carl Jung, we are what we do, not what we say we'll do. As educators we can tell our students we care about them every day, but the moment our behavior contradicts or is inconsistent with that message, they won't be able to hear as well whatever we say subsequently. "Many students victimized by trauma have been betrayed by adults who say one thing and act out another," explained Wolpow et al.

What we *do* always speaks that loudly, so what we do should be intentional, strategic. Accordingly, the rest of this chapter is dedicated to introducing additional evidence-based interventions and actionable strategies associated with trauma-informed teaching and administrating, most of which are very digestible and practical. Please note that these strategies are neither miraculous, instantaneous, nor absolute, and typically multiple strategies must be used consistently, concurrently, and confidently in order to see significant impact.

It's also important to note that most students experiencing complex trauma are never formally identified[43] and provided intensive support, particularly those experiencing race or poverty-based trauma. However, teachers should never assume a student has experienced trauma, get caught up in a student's trauma narrative (i.e., the emotion-laden details of a student's traumatic experience), or exert too much energy on attempting to informally determine which of their students have experienced trauma or not.

The following interventions and strategies are also applicable to promoting pro-academic behavior with students not necessarily impacted by complex trauma, so by using them with all students we're supporting every student without having to identify their individual level of trauma exposure.

Trauma-informed teaching and administrating features an intentional, practiced capacity to reduce retraumatization among trauma-impacted students by not participating in "trauma systems." By trauma system, we're referring to an abrupt, antagonistic psychoverbal interaction between a probably traumatized student and a teacher (or administrator) in which both concurrently struggle to self-regulate (i.e., not act out or antagonistically verbalize) negative emotions and impulsivity.

Experiencing complex trauma can instigate distinct, negative (or maladaptive), and enduring changes in a student's

---

[43] Part of being a trauma-informed school is screening your students to identify their individual level of trauma exposure. Trauma screening can be provided proactively to all students or selectively to those students notably displaying emotional dysregulation or hyperreactivity, impulsivity, and/or an overreliance on self-handicapping academic behavior that may possibly be associated with experiencing trauma. Possible screening tools include questionnaires, checklists, observations, and interviews, typically given by trained mental health personnel. Students identified as possibly or probably traumatized are then referred for a comprehensive trauma-informed mental health assessment and given appropriate access to therapy and other types of professional support as available.

194

psychological capacity to regulate their emotional reactions (i.e., traumatic stress response) to potentially threatening situations or events subsequently. Constant cortisol saturation, as aforementioned, significantly changes neural structures like the hippocampus and prefrontal cortex (PFC), both of which are gradually reduced in size and activity as cortisol annihilates hippocampus and PFC neurons via prolonged overactivation.

Conversely, continuous cortisol production increases the size and activity of the amygdala. The now hyperactive and hypertrophied amygdala promotes persistent states of hypervigilance and heightened emotional reactivity, even our traumatic stress response is exacerbated. The hypervigilant amygdala is constantly activating the traumatic stress response, and every activation makes a future activation (e.g., retraumatization in the classroom) much more likely.

Chronic traumatic stress strengthens the neural pathway between the amygdala and hippocampus and weakens the neural pathway between the hippocampus and prefrontal cortex. Consequently, our fight or flight response to perceived traumatic threats (or traumatic reminders) is drastically quickened because our ability to moderate this response is linked to the functional efficiency of the hippocampus and prefrontal cortex, both of which are neuronally atrophied by continuous cortisol saturation. In other words, an exaggerated traumatic stress response is a consequence of the brain changes brought about by experiencing chronic traumatic stress.

When it comes to teaching students probably impacted by complex trauma, it's noteworthy that oftentimes it's a negative teacher behavior or reaction, regardless of intentionality, that is perceived as an uncontrollable, potentially overwhelming psychological threat and triggers a traumatic stress response within the student's trauma-changed brain. The stress response prompts or exacerbates our student's inability to regulate negative emotions, impulsivity, and/or self-handicapping academic behaviors.

As the adult (and professional) in the room, it's our responsibility to stay in control of our own negative emotions when confronted with a student who is on the verge of or has already lost control of their negative emotions. It's our obligation as educators to respond strategically as opposed to reacting impulsively in order to deescalate the antagonism and get the focus back on learning. As trauma-informed administrators, it's important for us to provide appropriate support to classroom teachers as necessary (e.g., student may need to be removed temporarily from the classroom to calm down, reflect on their behavior, and/or receive logical consequence) and not penalize or negatively label them when your support is required.

Fundamental to our strategic response is deliberately and dependably avoiding "escalation responses," which include getting in a student's face, discrediting or humiliating the student, engaging in a power struggle with the student, asserting your authority over the student, yelling at the student, and/or rejecting the student (i.e., removal from class/school via office referral/suspension). Most escalation responses are inherently hostile and mimic behaviors exhibited during past trauma by presumably trustworthy authority figure (e.g., abusive parents get in the student's face, humiliate them, assert their authority over, or yell at them).

Escalation responses have a tendency to amplify the perception of a teacher or administrator as a potentially overwhelming (and, consequently, traumatic) psychological threat and the brain compensates by exaggerating the traumatic stress response, ultimately increasing the students' vulnerability to experiencing novel trauma (or retraumatization) during the trauma system.

Responding strategically enables us to teach the student how to self-regulate (or the value in self-regulating) their negative emotions by us *consistently* modeling self-regulation of our own. This is important for all students, but especially so for those experiencing complex trauma because their capacity to self-regulate has already been compromised by trauma.

Complex trauma "interferes with being fully present with a 'learning-ready' brain," explained Christopher Blodgett. Complex trauma can "impair the development of children's ability to regulate their emotions and to control impulsive behaviors," confirmed Susan Cole et al. "Reactions can be triggered in hypervigilant children if they feel they are being provoked or if something reminds them of the trauma. An incident or remark that might seem minor to a nontraumatized child may be perceived as threatening by a traumatized child, who then responds in a seemingly disproportionate way. It is helpful for teachers to know what triggers might cause a traumatized child to become hyperaroused or to reexperience a traumatic event in the classroom."

When students are in a triggered state, the learning-ready brain (led primarily by the logical prefrontal cortex, which maintains our ability to exert self-control over our thoughts, emotions, and behaviors) is subdued by the survival-only (overemotional amygdala-controlled) brain. Verbal warnings, threats, or even rational arguments posed by educators that make cognitive demands of their students' reason-based brain regions tend to escalate the situation (and perception of threat) as students are physiologically unable to access these regions when they are in a triggered state. The survival-only brain does not respond to words because it is wired to prioritize actions over words in moments of (physical or psychological) survival. It's typically what we do or how we react as opposed to what we say or listen to that saves our life (or self-concept), which is why words usually can't calm us down when triggered.

Much of the negative student behaviors we experience—particularly in high-poverty, high-minority classrooms—are actually consequences of chronic, yet unintentional, *retraumatization* in the classroom. Retraumatization, according to Karen Zgoda et al., is a "conscious or unconscious reminder of

197

past trauma that results in a re-experiencing of the initial trauma event. It can be triggered by a situation, an attitude or expression, or by certain environments that replicate the dynamics (loss of power/control/safety) of the original trauma"—this is referred to as a "trauma trigger."

A trauma trigger can pretty much be anything (a person, place, perception, behavior, situation) that somehow reminds you, knowingly or unknowingly, of a previous traumatic experience or how you felt or psychoemotionally reacted during the experience. These triggers can be terribly difficult to identify, anticipate, avoid, or control.

Teacher behaviors that typically become trauma triggers for students who have experienced trauma (especially when these behaviors are chronic) include being emotionally inconsistent or unstable; having poor classroom management; executing rough transitions between activities; humiliating students; yelling at, scolding, threatening, or arguing with students; being sarcastic; disregarding (i.e., overtly lowering their academic expectations of) disengaged, disruptive, or low-performing students; demonstrating bias or favoritism; lecturing too much (i.e., using whole-class lectures and discussions as their dominant teaching method); being overly strict and restrictive (i.e., having too many unnecessary classroom rules); engaging in racial microaggressions; and being hasty in referring students to office/administration (and as an administrator, being hasty in suspending or expelling students).

Accordingly, being a trauma-informed teacher requires a daily, reflection-based commitment to not commit/continue these behaviors.

There are moments when a student's behavioral reaction to a classroom situation or your own behavior seems especially inexplicable or inappropriate. In these moments, it is most likely that the situation or behavior has somehow triggered a traumatic stress response in that (apparently traumatized) student's brain. In these moments, it is critical that you (as probably the only trauma-informed person in the room) 1) identify the behavior for what it possibly is (and sometimes it won't necessarily be retraumatization) and 2) strategically encourage de-triggering[44].

When a student is retraumatized, the current experience (i.e., trauma trigger) provokes them to automatically feel or psychoemotionally react similarly to how they did during the past traumatic experience (or experiences). They are experiencing in that moment (in your classroom of all places!) some kind of perceived threat to their psychological (and sometimes even physical) well-being. And this perceived threat is accompanied by an abrupt inability to regulate their negative emotions (e.g., feeling overwhelmed, afraid, angry, rejected, helpless, trapped) or think or behave rationally.

All thought and behavior in that moment—even if disruptive or self-handicapping—is psychological (and sometimes even physical) survival-oriented. The student's primary concern in that moment (as opposed to learning from or listening to you) is somehow stopping the negative emotions associated with the perceived threat without having adequate access to those parts of the human brain that typically stop negative emotions. The reply then becomes using other/more negative emotions (and emotional behavior) to try to stop the negative emotions currently being experienced, which is akin to attempting to extinguish a housefire by using other/more fire.

At this point these students need to be de-triggered. Unfortunately, at this point most teachers (and remember, most teachers are not trauma-informed) respond with being emotionally inconsistent or unstable; having poor classroom management; executing rough transitions between activities; humiliating students; yelling at, scolding, threatening, or arguing with students; being sarcastic; disregarding (i.e., overtly lowering their academic expectations of) disengaged, disruptive, or low-performing

---

[44] De-triggering basically involves 1) identifying your trauma triggers (which assumes you are already cognizant of having experienced trauma) and 2) consciously deciding (and learning how) not to succumb to these triggers. Neither step is particularly easy, by the way.

students; demonstrating bias or favoritism; lecturing too much (i.e., using whole-class lectures and discussions as their dominant teaching method); being overly strict and restrictive (i.e., having too many unnecessary classroom rules); engaging in racial microaggressions; and being hasty in referring students to office/administration.

Yes, this means that students who are experiencing retraumatization in our classrooms are oftentimes responded to with additional trauma triggers; instead of de-triggering, *we* are retriggering. And yes, this is a bad thing (and a worse thing if we continue doing it after being informed).

Ideally, we'd like to prevent retraumatization in our classrooms. While complete prevention is outside of our control, *reducing* retraumatization in our classrooms is something we can control mostly by decreasing those aforementioned teacher behaviors that typically become trauma triggers for students who have experienced trauma—especially when you consider that most of the negative student behavior we're reacting to is more so annoying (to us) than malignant.[45]

Accordingly, we'd recommend at least regulating a lot more intentionally is yelling at, scolding, threatening, or arguing with our students. The level of hostility with which a teacher verbally reacts to negative (but not necessarily life threatening) student behavior should never be so egregious that it becomes a trauma trigger; yet somehow this has become the norm, particularly in high-poverty, high-minority classrooms.

Children who have not had the opportunity to form secure attachments with the adults in their lives because of past trauma may perceive all adults as potential psychological (and perhaps even physical) threats. This perception automatically jeopardizes the functionality of their student-educator relationships; a student

---

[45] Not sweating the small stuff helps us to reduce those teacher behaviors that may be trauma triggers for our students. "Learning to stop sweating the small stuff," explained Carlson, "involves deciding what things to engage in and what things to ignore."

won't/can't learn from you very efficiently once their brain prioritizes reacting to you as a threat (because their stress response is now active). Traumatized children can be uniquely "sensitive to nonverbal cues, such as tone of voice, volume, posturing, and facial expressions," explained Elizabeth Keller-Dupree, particularly cues indicative of confrontation. So, once you repeatedly display cues that are (or can be perceived as) unnecessarily confrontational (e.g., yelling at, scolding, threatening, or arguing with), these cues can confirm (to them) that you are what they thought you were: just another threat.

Accordingly, as clarified by Susan Cole et al., "many traumatized children adopt behavioral coping mechanisms that can frustrate educators and evoke exasperated reprisals, reactions that both strengthen expectations of confrontation and danger and reinforce a negative self-image." However, their (potential or actual) trauma doesn't somehow excuse the hostility with which we communicate or attempt to manage our classrooms. If anything, it should motivate us (as educators aspiring to successfully educate all students) to not behave in a way that we become seen as just another adult threat to not trust and act out towards or avoid.

Requiring trauma-informed educators to stop (or at least strategically minimize) yelling at, scolding, threatening, or arguing with students should not insinuate a request to lower their academic and behavioral expectations of potentially traumatized students. It *is* a request to change how we communicate and enforce higher expectations for all students. Educators who practice deescalating their reactions to negative student behavior enable student-educator relationships based on trust and unconditional positive regard to evolve organically.

For many students who have experienced trauma and trauma-based maladaptive neuroplasticity, a teacher yelling at, scolding, threatening, or arguing with them merely escalates or perpetuates their negative classroom behaviors, so why would we continue to not practice a less confrontational style of responding? Teacher

201

ignorance (of trauma-based student behavior and trauma-informed responses), indifference, inflexibility, incompetence, implicit bias, ill intentions (we're assuming that was not a rhetorical question—and we really enjoy alliteration).

Being trauma-informed means actively changing how we perceive students and react to their negative classroom behaviors. It's means, explained Sandra Bloom, learning and adopting strategies that enable us to shift the basis of our response from "what is wrong with you?" to "what happened to you and how can I help?" when addressing disruptive or self-handicapping student behaviors. Making this shift can "be very hard for teachers, some of whom have been exposed to trauma themselves," noted Pamela Cantor.

Becoming trauma-informed, explained Krasnoff, is a "long, gradual process, but once the focus has shifted, there is an immediate change in school culture from reactive to proactive (for example, the staff stops responding punitively to students' challenges and behaviors). As the culture shifts toward trauma sensitivity, teachers feel more aware, as well as empowered to intervene constructively. They realize that supporting students socially, emotionally, and behaviorally will only improve their ability to focus on academics."

With regard to their impulsive, disruptive, or self-handicapping behavior, respond to your students, especially those showing signs of possible trauma, by offering choices and consequences as opposed to hostility and confrontation (which may be seen as threatening). Publicized, predetermined (as opposed to reactive, frustration-based) choices and consequences, when used properly, enable educators to drastically reduce the need for hostility and confrontation. And whenever choices need to be delivered impromptu, say it calmly, kindly, discreetly, succinctly, with brief but direct eye contact, and then give space to allow for reflection. Trauma typically involves uncontrollability; offering students choices and consequences could help restore a trauma-compromised sense of safety and self-efficacy via controllability.

"Children who experience consequences learn that they have control over the consequences by exerting control over their behaviors. In other words," observed Cindy Stauffer, "children learn they are free to choose their behaviors, as long as they are willing to accept the consequences," which may also motivate those experiencing trauma to be more cognizant of the impact of trauma-based maladaptive neuroplasticity on their behavior. Consequences promote more positive neuroplasticity and are less likely to retraumatize than punishment (and exclusionary discipline) when used strategically.

Trauma-informed teachers and administrators do not discuss consequences with students whose brains are still triggered into survival mode; it's more efficient to wait a bit for them to calm down. Consequences make cognitive demands of our students' reason-based brain regions (led primarily by the prefrontal cortex), which means they also tend to escalate the perception of (us as) threat as students are physiologically unable to access these regions when they are in a triggered state. As aforementioned, the survival-only brain does not respond to words because it is wired to prioritize actions over words in moments of (physical or psychological) survival.

Once students are ready to discuss consequences, the consequences we offer should be proportional to the negative student behavior, enforceable, and applied consistently. They should not be cumulative or threatening. "Threats teach children to be afraid rather than problem-solve and reason-out the connection between behaviors and consequences." Consequences are used in conjunction with preestablished classroom rules or norms, and should reference the rules or norms when a specific one is violated. Offer multiple consequences and allow students to choose from them. Or whenever possible, let students create some consequences for you to choose from. Doing so offers the additional abovementioned benefit of controllability, but remember to be firm and fair and don't argue or negotiate with student.

There is no more efficient evidence-based intervention associated with childhood trauma-based maladaptive neuroplasticity than a safe, positive, and consistent relationship with an adult. Students impacted by trauma typically have not experienced many other positive relationships with adults. Accordingly, our goal as trauma-informed educators should be to establish a relationally based classroom and school. A relationally based classroom and school is based on the belief that underachieving students, including those experiencing complex trauma, will try their hardest to regulate negative emotions and impulsivity and overcome their overreliance on self-handicapping academic behaviors for teachers and administrators they have established a safe, positive, and consistent relationship with. These students are most likely to continually try to be "good students" by practicing more pro-academic behaviors, taking more academic risks, and relying on their positive student-educator relationships, and by doing so, the neural circuitry for those activities begin to strengthen as the brain rewires itself through positive experience.

It may sound corny, but "sometimes," to quote Rebecca Rider, "all it takes to change a child's life is a relationship." The relationships we establish with our potentially traumatized students may become the most influential of all our students with regard to setting the overall tone of our classrooms. How strategically we respond to the impulsive and self-handicapping behaviors of our potentially traumatized students has the most influence on these relationships. The more strategic our response, the more likely our potentially traumatized students will trust that we are not a threat and it's safe to allow us to teach them. The more student-educator trust is established, the less our potentially traumatized students will have to rely on impulsive and self-handicapping behaviors to avoid the lingering threat of retraumatization. The fewer of these behaviors we have to encounter, the more effort we can then exert on higher quality instruction and ultimately greater student achievement.

By intentionally creating and sustaining positive, appropriately transparent, mutually respectful, and rejection-free student-educator relationships, we create the conditions necessary to significantly reverse trauma-based maladaptive neuroplasticity. According to feedback from students compiled by Mary Fecser, there are certain straightforward tendencies or practices common among educators most effective in forming this type of relationship. They tend to "maintain a calm but confident demeanor; run a structured and predictable classroom following regular routines; actively involve the students in the lessons; they're patient; they're funny; and they listen."

Use humor routinely to inject positive emotional experiences like happiness, enthusiasm, enjoyment, and calm into your classroom and school. When our students see us laugh and smile more, mirror neurons in their brain encourage them to laugh and smile more too and better regulate negative emotional experiences like criticism, conflict, disappointment, and distrust. And research confirms that happier students feel safer and are more academically motivated, resilient, and successful. Tanner Wallace et al. explained that "teachers' use of humor played a role in how students perceived being known by that teacher. To effectively use humor required shared experience and a certain level of nuanced knowledge of that student's personal history. In turn, a kind of reciprocity in attention and respect developed between students and their teachers."

It's often not acknowledged as such, but greeting your students before class or school or in the hallway during transitions by name with a smile (adding a special handshake or dap is always optional) is one of the easiest trauma-informed strategies. As often as possible, when greeting attempt to engage students one-on-one (especially those you suspect may be experiencing trauma based on ongoing classroom behavior) in compassionate, positive miniconservations[46] about their interests, future plans, experiences, successes, concerns, etc. Fecser explained that children carrying the "effects of past trauma feel as though they have not been seen or heard appropriately by people who were supposed to care for and protect them. The educator can become that missing person." Doing so creates a more effectual student-educator relationship, demonstrates unconditional positive regard, and diminishes the anticipation of the educator as a potential threat. Students may seem hesitant to engage in these greetings and mini-conversations initially, but as they become normalized and expected, students will also see them as safe, genuine, and appealing.

As humans, we all yearn to be seen, heard, and valued by others (and as children or adolescents, we yearn to be seen, heard, and valued by adults especially). For those of us who have experienced complex trauma, this yearning is even greater because trauma jeopardizes our natural trust in others and confidence in the likelihood that these needs could be met. When these needs are met, explained Tiffany Schiffman, "the brain will respond with physical changes and the creation of new neural networks." Greeting our students as aforedescribed is a simple way to meet this need for them, reverse possible trauma-based maladaptive neuroplasticity. "Secure attachment and psychological safety result in the release of neurotransmitters that build new neuronal networks that actually help move the student's thinking from the limbic system (where reactivity to emotions occurs) into the frontal cortex where higher level cognition—abstract and reflective thinking—occur. With a secure attachment in place, it is then that the teacher can provide challenge by gently questioning the student's unhelpful assumptions, beliefs and behaviors while inviting him or her to explore and consider more useful alternatives."

---

[46]   Be prepared to offer additional time as needed based on your typical availability (or in urgent instances, work with administration to make yourself or another supportive adult available immediately.)

Don't forget to demonstrate *unconditional* positive regard. Quite frankly, this one is going to be tough because it's most often misperceived as being indifferent or intimidated. Actually, unconditional positive regard requires an educator being remarkably compassionate and courageous (and having an exceptional capacity to stay calm and committed to unconditionality when students are triggered or for whatever reason is exhibiting disruptive, impulsive, or self-handicapping behavior). Wolpow et al. defined unconditional positive regard as "the various ways an adult shows sustained kindness and genuine respect for students as human beings. Students struggling with the trauma don't need another adult to tell them what is wrong with them. What they do need, what helps them thrive, is an adult who treats them with simple sustained kindness," shows respect for them, and values them exactly the way they are.

"Traumatic events make it difficult for children to trust, to feel worthy, take initiative, and form relationships." Educators expressing unconditional positive regard can make these actions less difficult by demonstrating that "adults can consistently act and respond with positive regard."

Talia Kraemer and Eliza Patten noted that students who experiencing trauma often expect adult "relationships to reinforce negative beliefs they have developed about themselves and others; for example, that they are inherently unlikeable or 'bad,' or that adults are untrustworthy and will inevitably hurt them. They are more likely to be hypervigilant in social interactions and to misread facial or verbal cues as negative" because they expect negativity. They tend to "push the adult away or provoke an adverse response. Students may be modeling how they have been treated in past relationships or trying to achieve control by bringing about negative treatment that they consider inevitable." Or these students may be engaging in negative behaviors just to test "whether you will ultimately disappoint and reject them, as other adults have done." Accordingly, trauma-informed educators anticipate and do not allow any of these possibly unfavorable

207

reactions, especially when trauma-based, to excuse or create conditionality.

Consistently confirm that your classroom/school is a safe space (i.e., reduced conditions of threat and retraumatization) with your words, actions, and responses. This can be accomplished, according to Keller-Dupree, by "reestablishing a routine for children, including consistent rules and expectations, reliability and predictability, and availability of adult support." Under conditions of threat the amygdala basically takes over the brain, noted Fecser, "bypassing the prefrontal cortex and preventing real learning from taking place," particularly in students experiencing trauma-based neuroplasticity (and a consequently hyperactive and hypertrophied amygdala). However, when these students feel safe, their amygdalar response can be held in check, enabling them to better regulate negative emotions, impulsivity, and their overreliance on self-handicapping academic behaviors.

Teachers (and administrators) that "maintain a calm but confident demeanor provide the sense that they are in control" and the classroom (and school) is a safe place. Instability, inconsistency, insecurity, or impulsivity on our part implies a greater possibility of threat and retraumatization. In other words, teachers and administrators who cannot maintain a calm assertiveness or regulate their own stress-related behavior also presumably cannot keep their students safe (especially psychologically). Students experiencing trauma are uniquely hypersensitive to any signs of these shortcomings and will neither trust you to keep them safe nor *waste time* sustaining a positive relationship with an adult who can't keep them safe.

Trauma-informed educators "set and enforce limits in a consistent way that provides high expectations for all students," observed Maura McInerney and Amy McKlindon. "Maintaining consistent expectations, limits, and routines sends the message that the student is worthy of continued unconditional positive regard and attention. In addition, consistency in the classroom helps

208

students differentiate between the arbitrary rules that led to their abuse and the purposeful ones that assure their safety."

Consistency, predictability, and routine are all essential to establishing relationally based classrooms and schools where all students can feel safe. It's easier for students, particularly those experiencing complex trauma, to trust us as educators (and our capacity to keep them safe) when they know what to expect from us. Establishing and enforcing (and discussing the rationale for our) coherent routines, rules, protocols, and incentives; efficiently managing student-to-student stressors (e.g., embarrassment, harassment, bullying, cyberbullying, verbal conflict, threats of violence); being consistent in our expectations, consequences, and responses; and avoiding humiliating, threatening, yelling at, or arguing with students creates a learning environment where all students can feel safe.

We also recommend formally teaching students about complex trauma, trauma-based neuroplasticity, racial literacy, racial stigma, racial inequality, racial microaggressions, race-based traumatic stress, the structural causes of intergenerational poverty in America, poverty as stigma, and the poverty mindset. "Black children and adolescents are particularly vulnerable," observed Maryam Jernigan et al., to "racial trauma because they may not have yet developed a sophisticated cognitive understanding or the affective language with which to process the ongoing effects of racism." A similar vulnerability has manifested itself with regard to students experiencing intergenerational poverty.

Key to being a fully trauma-informed educator is accepting that these topics can no longer be considered taboo, too uncomfortable, or somehow not worth the instructional time. To help our students cope with potential race and poverty-based trauma, we owe them a safe, structured, and informed space to have honest conversations about their stressful experiences related to being Black or poor. Even if these are just mini-discussions reliably added to traditional lessons, merely knowing these potentially adverse phenomena *by name* can have a tremendous impact on our Black and poor students' capacity to adaptively self-protect.

Explicitly teaching specific academic or study skills (e.g., using guided notes, graphic organizers, reading comprehension strategies, building academic vocabulary, working memory) along with other 21st century success skills is also ridiculously valuable. Oftentimes, Black and poor students (regardless of their trauma exposure) are overly penalized and hastily labeled for not already being proficient in these skills, but few educators ever invest the effort to teach these skills. One evidence-based strategy we recommend is including student workshops focusing on teaching specific academic and 21st century success skills as a Tier 2 MTSS intervention.

Our underlying goal as trauma-informed educators should be to identify and provide what a student may need in order to no longer feel compelled to perform problematic behavior—not just illogically punish behavior possibly trauma-based because it's expedient to do so. Accountability must somehow be balanced with an understanding of trauma-based behavior. Most of this effort is strategically building their capacity to better regulate negative emotions, impulsivity, and their overreliance on self-handicapping academic behaviors (because all students would rather be successful). And appreciating that building this capacity (and changing the behavior) is resource-intensive, time-consuming, and somewhat speculative.

Made in the USA
San Bernardino, CA
06 February 2020